GW01607781

THE MASTER GARDENER'S GUIDE TO

LAWN CARE

All you'll ever need to know about creating and maintaining a healthy lawn

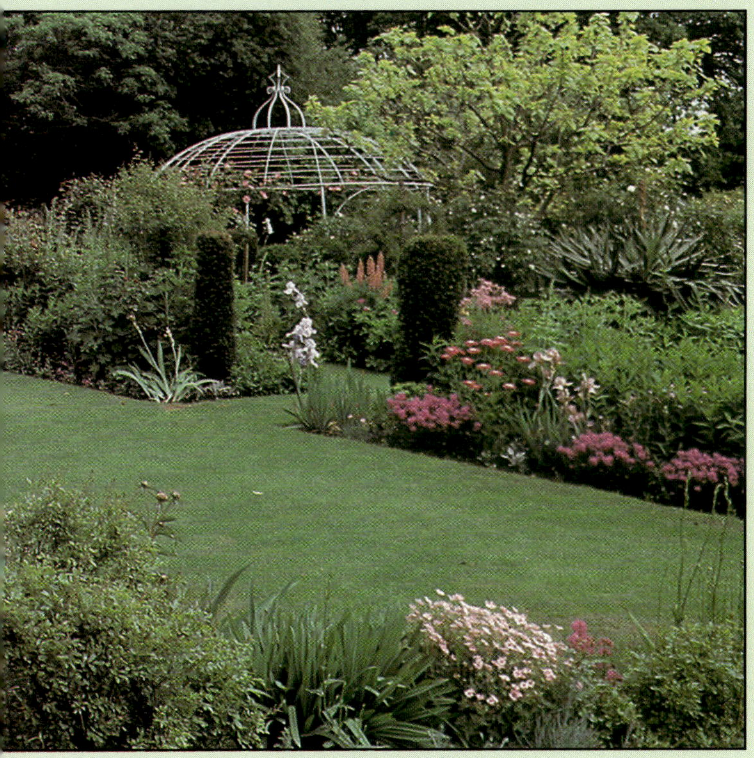

ROBERT PALIN

Published by Salamander Books Limited
LONDON

A SALAMANDER BOOK

Salamander House,
27 Old Gloucester Street,
London WC1N 3AF,
United Kingdom.

ISBN 0 86101 169 4

Distributed by the UK by
Hodder & Stoughton Services,
P.O. Box 6, Mill Road,
Dunton Green, Sevenoaks,
Kent TN13 2XX.

Credits
Editor: John Woodward
Colour reproductions:
Rodney Howe Ltd.

Filmset: Modern Text Ltd.
Printed in Belgium by
Henri Proost & Cie, Turnhout.

AUTHOR

Robert Palin is an agronomist with over 40 years' experience of advising on turf and lawn care. He is an Executive Director of Suttons Seeds Ltd, a company which specialises in grass seeds, and in this capacity he travels internationally to advise on the establishment and maintenance of golf courses, sports grounds and amenity lawns. He has written and contributed to several authoritative books on the subject, and has lectured at the Regent Street Polytechnic, London, and the Royal Botanic Gardens at Kew.

Consultant

Ann Bonar has been a horticultural writer and consultant for more than 20 years, and has written many books on various aspects of gardening. She is a regular contributor to a variety of gardening periodicals and trade journals, and has taken part in a number of gardening programmes broadcast by the BBC. For 12 years she has answered readers' queries sent in to a leading British weekly gardening magazine.

CONTENTS

Introduction 8

Making a Lawn

Design 11

Grasses 16

Alternatives to grass 20

The soil 22

Drainage 24

Levelling and landscaping 26

Maintenance

Mowing 36

Edging 40

Feeding the lawn 42

Irrigation 46

Aeration 48

Repairs and renovation 50

Common lawn weeds 54

Dealing with weeds 58

Lawn pests 60

Grass diseases 62

Mosses, algae, lichens and fungi 64

Equipment

Mowers 66

Mower maintenance 68

Lawncare tools 70

Seasonal care

Autumn and winter 72

Spring and summer 74

Index 76

INTRODUCTION

The lawn has become an essential part of the modern garden. It provides a place to relax in the sun, work in the open air, and admire the results of the gardener's labour. Children have a place to play which will absorb the bumps, and which keeps them out of doors and out of danger. A lawn is relatively easy to keep in good condition, and amply repays the effort by providing a perfect foil for flowers, shrubs and trees. Few gardeners who have had a lawn could imagine their garden without it.

Until the invention of the lawnmower in 1830 the lawn was a luxury to be enjoyed by the wealthy few, who could afford to pay a skilled worker to mow it with a scythe every two weeks. Considering the rough-hewn effect that this could produce, it was perhaps as well that the prevailing fashion in the 18th century was for naturalistic landscape gardening.

The advent of the lawnmower made it relatively easy to achieve the neat finish we now expect, and made the lawn a practical proposition for the ordinary gardener. Today many gardens consist almost entirely of grass, and mowing the lawn is, for some, the only garden task they undertake.

One of the points in favour of a lawn is that, in temperate climates, grass grows with great, indeed embarrassing speed. It is difficult to keep it from escaping the boundaries of the lawn and overrunning the flower-beds and borders. One result of this is that many lawn owners regard grass as quite self-sufficient, needing

only the occasional trim to keep it in order. In fact, over the years a lawn can develop a wide variety of problems resulting from the wrong type of grass, poor soil, hard wear, inadequate drainage or fertility, or attack by pests and diseases. As the grass fails, its place is taken by a host of weeds, coarse grasses and mosses which spoil the texture and colour of the turf.

This can be prevented by taking care, when making a new lawn, to choose the right grasses for the soil conditions, and by careful preparation of the site. There are a variety of grasses suitable for specific conditions of soil and aspect, and some which will tolerate harder wear than others. Good soil preparation ensures healthy grass throughout the life of the lawn, discourages invaders such as weeds, pests and fungus, and reduces the need to be constantly feeding, watering and aerating the turf. Care in lawn design and the placing of borders will reduce the time spent mowing and trimming edges.

If the lawn is already made, careful analysis and treatment of the various problems will ensure that, in a year or two, the turf is returned to an acceptable condition. The level of regular maintenance can then be reduced to a minimum so that the lawn can be properly appreciated as a recreation area, and enjoyed as a beautiful garden feature in its own right.

Below: *Beautiful, practical and labour-saving, a well-made lawn is an asset to any garden.*

Making a Lawn

Creating an attractive and useful lawn involves more than simply spreading seed or turf over a patch of bare earth. The lawn has to be carefully designed to suit the limitations of the site. The ground needs careful preparation to ensure a firm, well-drained and fertile foundation, and the grasses must be chosen to suit the soil and the way the finished lawn will be used.

DESIGN

Designing and making a lawn from scratch may seem more difficult than taking over a lawn which is already estabished, and altering it to suit your needs and preferences. In fact, grafting new design ideas on to an existing lawn and its surroundings can result in a lawn which is awkward and unmanageable. It is nearly always easier, and more satisfactory in the long run, to do away with the existing lawn and its problems—thin turf, bad drainage, weeds and pests—and start again. It is quite easy to produce a new lawn from seed or turf, and you are able to plan it from the bare soil stage to take into account the exact requirements of you and your family.

When you sit down at the drawing-board, or at any rate with a pencil and a sheet of squared paper, what should you consider when producing your initial design? First of all, the design and location of the lawn will be influenced by the size of the garden. Unless the plot is very large, the options will be some-

Below: *A well-designed lawn is attractive, useful and easy to maintain, and provides a perfect background for the other features of the garden.*

what limited—and ninety per cent of lawns are sited in small rectangular gardens which also have to contain flower beds, a vegetable patch, a garden shed, a coal bunker or oil tank, and an area for the compost heap and bonfire.

Despite these restrictions there is no need for the lawn to follow the shape of the garden. For instance, you can set it diagonally on the site, put it at one end, or place it crosswise to take up half the garden. You can cut it in two to provide an element of surprise, and use a hedge or a line of informal flowering shrubs as a divider—or simply indicate the division with the help of one or two small trees.

Above: *An island bed planted with shrubs will divide the lawn in two, adding style and variety to an otherwise standard garden rectangle.*

The lines of a square or rectangular lawn give a distinctive formal tone to the garden, but it is essential to keep the edges immaculately clean-cut, free of fringes, and absolutely ruler straight. It is worth remembering this at the design stage. Informal shapes are not quite so demanding, and irregular curved edges have a different but considerable appeal of their own. If your preference is for curves, however, try to make them gentle and sweeping, rather than tight or

Above top: *the flamboyance of flowering border plants is enhanced by the crisp lines of a formal, square-cut lawn, but neat edging is essential.*

Above: *Graceful flowing curves provide interest at the lawn edge and, if well designed, can increase the apparent size of a small garden plot.*

complex, because intricate shapes are time-consuming and irritating to mow.

The position and aspect of the lawn will be affected by other factors besides the size and shape of the garden. Anything which casts shade has to be taken into account. Tall buildings and fences, for example, create shadows of varying intensity which may affect grass growth and make the finished lawn less inviting. Trees, although they add beauty to the garden and the lawn, may exclude sunlight and tend to take an unfair share of available moisture and plant food; some also create problems with autumn leaf-fall.

The lie of the land can be important. A slightly sloping site of about 1 in 85 is permissible, but anything more will make mowing difficult, even if you use a hover mower. If the only site available has a pronounced slope, you should consider terracing, or a major levelling exercise.

Features within the area of the

lawn should be decided on and designed in advance of construction. You may want a pool or a fountain, a herbaceous border or island beds, a barbecue, or permanent seats or benches. It is easier to see their effect on the appearance of the lawn if they are drawn in on a scale plan first. Such features should be built before the lawn is laid, otherwise the grass can be badly damaged during construction, especially if it is grown from seed.

When considering the shape and style of the lawn, bear in mind that containers, garden furniture and tiny flower-beds make mowing difficult, and that areas of grass between flower beds should be a little more than two mowers wide. If you put stepping-stone paths in the lawn, ensure that each stone is set slightly below the lawn's surface, and be sure that the edges of the lawn can be mown without damaging the mower or nearby plants or fences.

SOIL AND DRAINAGE

The type of soil in the garden is of vital importance as it affects the choice of grass species and therefore, to some extent, the use which can be made of the lawn. A heavy soil which tends to be moist will need a coarser grass seed mixture than one which is light and drains well, and it may not be suitable for a high-quality lawn unless the soil characteristics are modified. Soils with strongly acid or alkaline reactions will require special seed mixtures, and these may not fit in with your original plans.

If the soil is particularly badly drained, or if the garden is at a low point so that the water table is very near the surface, it may not be possible to have a lawn at all unless you are prepared to accept moss and some weeds as permanent residents. A lot can be done by soil improvement in advance, and the laying of drains under the lawn.

Above: *The function of the lawn must be decided at the outset. An ornamental lawn such as this will need careful preparation and the right choice of seed.*

LAWN TYPES

The way the lawn is to be used will have a major bearing on the choice of seed mixture or turf. Many lawns have to take a good deal of punishment; they have to be able to stand up to children's cricket matches or tricycle races, dogs and cats, guinea-pigs and rabbits—even ducks and geese. For such a lawn a mixture of tufted and creeping grasses is best, especially if the creeping species produce underground stems, or rhizomes. These modified stems surface at regular intervals, producing leaves to replace those destroyed by hard use. There is no reason why such play lawns should not be both tough and good-looking if the right grasses are used, and allowed to become properly established before being subjected to wear and tear.

The utility or fine lawn is also hard wearing, but more luxurious in appearance. It is made up of a mixture of finer cultivars of the same grass species, and if properly maintained, the turf will be similar to that of a tennis court or the average golf green. Such a lawn has many uses and is excellent for afternoon tea, barbecue parties, clock golf, croquet, and to show off flower-beds and the house to advantage.

The ornamental lawn is for the perfectionist, and should be absolutely without blemish. It should be subjected to very little traffic (though it may be used for sunbathing!), and will require loving care throughout the year to create the texture of a championship bowling green. A light to medium soil is ideal for such a lawn, but heavy clays can be improved in advance sufficiently to support the fine grasses which are used.

GRASSES

Of the 10,000 or so species of grass which occur worldwide, relatively few are suitable for lawn turf. Of these, each has different qualities, and each is suited to particular conditions. It is important to choose with care if you are to produce a good-looking lawn which is suitable for your purpose.

CHOOSING A SEED MIXTURE

The choice of grasses for the new lawn will depend partly on soil type and climate, and partly on how the lawn is to be used. If it is to be purely ornamental, then the finest grasses should be used regardless of durability. If it is intended for hard use by children, the turf must be as strong as possible, or it will be quickly disfigured by bare patches. Most gardeners opt for a compromise—a utility lawn which looks attractive but is tough enough to stand moderately hard wear.

The four most important grass types used in lawn turf mixtures in temperate climates are the bent grasses, meadow grasses, fescues and ryegrasses. Bent grasses (*Agrostis*) are all perennials which produce creeping underground stems (rhizomes) or creeping surface stems (stolons). They are fine-leaved, and reasonably durable. Meadow grasses (*Poa*) may be annuals or perennials. Some are tufted (non-creeping) and others spread by rhizomes or stolons, forming a hard-wearing turf. The fescues (*Festuca*) are fine-leaved grasses, ideal for high-quality turf, whereas rye-grasses (*Lolium*) are often coarse, vigorous grasses, used for durability rather than show.

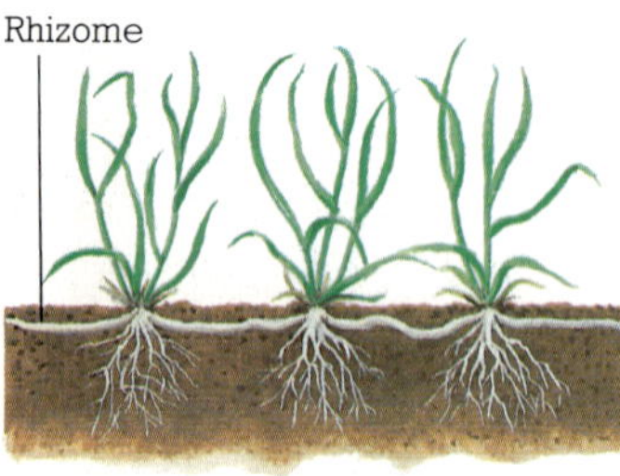

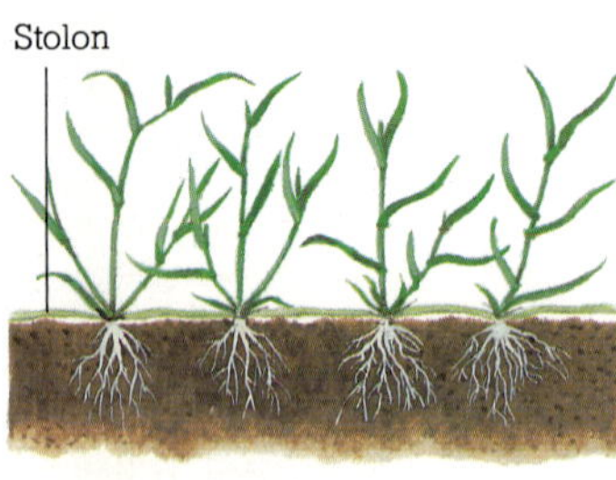

Left: *Smooth-stalked meadow grass (top) has underground rhizomes. Creeping bent (centre) has surface-rooting stolons. Chewing's fescue (bottom) is a tufted, non-creeping grass.*

LAWN SPECIES

Browntop
Agrostis tenuis
Used extensively in lawn grass mixtures, browntop has spear-shaped narrow leaves, and produces both stolons and short rhizomes. It grows well in most soils, including acid heathlands and moorlands, and it stands up well to traffic when properly established. *Agrostis castellana* is a fine-leaved form.

Creeping bent
Agrostis stolonifera
Similar in leaf shape and size to browntop, but with rather paler coloration, creeping bent produces very leafy stolons which form a surface mat and help to

stabilise sloping areas. It is not considered very suitable for fine lawns in temperate regions, but it is widely used in Mediterranean countries. Creeping bent has no special soil preferences, but it needs plenty of moisture or it forms a rather stemmy surface thatch.

Smooth stalked meadow grass
Poa pratensis
This is the Kentucky blue grass of America, so called because of its blue-green foliage. The leaves have parallel sides, and distinctively hooded tips, and the plant produces robust rhizomes which reinforce the soil and produce a dense sward at the surface. It does not tolerate close mowing, and takes time to become established, but even so it is a useful ingredient of grass seed mixtures for hard wear, particularly on lighter soils.

Rough stalked meadow grass
Poa trivialis
Quicker to establish itself than *Poa pratensis*, and capable of growing well in the shade of buildings or trees, this is a useful grass for such problem areas of the lawn. It has very dark green foliage and parallel-sided leaves which taper to a sharp point. The upper leaf surface is always dull and the underside is shiny. The plants need a moist heavy soil to do well, and produce stolons under ideal conditions.

Below: *A utility seed mixture will produce a good looking yet hard wearing turf.*

GRASSES

Creeping red fescue
Festuca rubra rubra
A very useful grass, particularly for drier soils, this has tightly inrolled bristle-like leaves and produces rhizomes. There are both slender and coarse varieties, but only the slender cultivars are useful for lawns. *Festuca litoralis* is a very slender type.

Chewing's fescue
Festuca rubra commutata
This is another very fine-bladed grass, with tightly inrolled leaves which give it a bristle-like appearance. A tufted plant with no stolons or rhizomes, it produces a dense compact sward, especially when combined with *Festuca rubra rubra* or *Agrostis tenuis.* It does best on lighter soils, but is quite adaptable and will grow in both acid and alkaline conditions.

Hard fescue
Festuca longifolia
Bluish-green or grey with very narrow leaves, hard fescue has a preference for well-drained stony or sandy soil. It can be particularly recommended for chalk.

Fine-leaved fescue
Festuca tenuifolia
This has very tightly inrolled, almost hairlike leaves, even narrower than those of hard fescue. The plant thrives on dry soils and is very tolerant of shade if it is not closely mown.

Crested dogstail
Cynosurus cristatus
Particularly useful for chalky or limestone soils, this grass has very dark green leaves with parallel sides. They are dull on the upper surface and glossy below, and grow very densely.

Perennial ryegrass
Lolium perenne
Many dwarf, leafy varieties of this hard-wearing grass have been developed for lawns, and the coarser types which needed frequent mowing are rarely used now. Versatile and quick to establish itself, ryegrass is best sown as part of a mixture; used alone it forms an open sward which invites invasion by moss and weeds. It has parallel-sided dark green leaves which are glossy beneath and dull above.

Above: *An ornamental lawn made of the finest grasses will show off other garden plants to advantage.*

Timothy
Phleum pratense
This is a hard-wearing, tufted grass, too coarse for the ornamental lawn but useful when durability is essential. Timothy has leaves which are widest at the base, gradually narrowing to the tip, greyish-green in colour and rough to the touch. The stem has a bulbous base, and sometimes a chain of such bulbils may develop. Lesser timothy (*Phleum bertolonii*) is similar, but has finer leaves which make it more suitable for lawns.

WEED GRASSES

Easily distinguished by their coarser foliage and poor colour, weed grasses can be difficult to eradicate. Chemical treatments are impractical, because of the risk of killing the lawn grasses; if the lawn is badly infested it may have to be completely remade.

Annual meadowgrass
Poa annua
This is generally considered to be a weed, although it is often tolerated in lawns and sports grounds. The flower heads have short stems, and often escape cutting until they have set seed; these are spread by mowing, and the plant rapidly colonises bare areas. Sensitive to drought, it changes colour during its short life from bright green to yellow, then dies.

Yorkshire fog
Holcus lanatus
A hairy perennial with greyish-green foliage and pink-striped off-white basal sheaths to the stems, Yorkshire fog can be a serious nuisance in fine turf. It may be discouraged by slashing with a sharp knife before mowing.

Creeping soft grass
Holcus mollis
Very similar in appearance to Yorkshire fog, this weed grass produces tough rhizomes which, if cut, produce new plants. Because of this, slashing is worse than useless; the offending patches have to be completely cut out or disposed of by localised chemical treatment.

Couch grass
Agropyron repens
An extensively creeping perennial, with very dark green foliage and large rhizomes which are easily broken; the broken pieces then grow into new plants. Land infested with couch grass must be carefully cleared, preferably chemically, before putting down to lawn.

ALTERNATIVES TO GRASS

A lawn does not have to be made of grass. Many other plants will tolerate being mown and walked on, and often become weeds of grass turf. If they are encouraged to grow together to form a lawn, it is the invading grass which is treated as a weed.

HERB LAWNS

Low-growing broadleaved herbs have been used for centuries to form lawns. Aromatic plants such as chamomile, pennyroyal and thyme are particularly attractive, releasing their fragrance as they are walked on.

The lawn site should be prepared as for grass, and a fine seedbed will be needed. With some species, seedlings transplanted into the lawn bed will give better results. Such lawns will not stand very hard wear, and although they react reasonably well to mowing, none of the common herbs will tolerate close cutting. Set the mowing height at about ¾in (20mm).

Weeds can be a problem in herb lawns. Selective weed-killers cannot distinguish between broadleaved weeds and lawn herbs, and will kill both while leaving any invading grasses untouched. Hand weeding is often the only solution.

SUITABLE PLANTS

Clovers

Of the many species of clover available, three in particular are used: wild white clover (*Trifolium repens*), yellow suckling clover (*Trifolium dubium*) and yellow trefoil (*Medicago lupulina*). If they are planted individually or as a mixture, a seeding rate of ¼-½oz per yd² (9-17g per m²) is sufficient. To sow with grass, use ½oz of clover seed mixed with the same amount of grass seed per square yard (17g of clover plus 17g of grass per m²). The clovers prefer alkaline soils and are best sown in April, or July to August.

Yarrow

Achillea millefolium

Normally regarded as a weed in

Below: *Chamomile grows into a compact sward of fern-like plants which release a sweet fragrance at every step.*

lawns, yarrow can produce quite a good lawn itself if regularly mown. The seed is very small and needs to be mixed with sand, before sowing at a rate of ¼oz per yd² (9g per m²).

Chamomile
Anthemis nobilis
Chamomile is a small fern-like creeping plant, which emits a sweet scent when mown or walked on. Popular for centuries as a lawn plant, it remains the most widely-used non-grass species. It is best sown in boxes or beds, and planted out when the seedlings are big enough to handle. The plants should be spaced at 4-6in (10-13cm) intervals; they need "topping" when they are about 3in (75mm) tall, and the height should be reduced gradually to about ¾in (20mm).

Pennyroyal
Mentha pulegium
Another popular lawn herb, which smells of peppermint when bruised. Like chamomile it is best raised in beds or boxes and transplanted; the seedlings should be spaced 4-6in (10-13cm) apart on the lawn site.

Below: *Thyme is available in a variety of colours which can be blended into a very attractive aromatic herb lawn.*

Wild thyme
Thymus serpyllum
A well-known aromatic herb which forms natural lawns in close-cropped wild turf. It can be raised in beds or boxes and planted out when large enough to handle, or sown directly into a prepared seedbed.

Kidney weed
Dichondra repens
An excellent ground-cover plant used extensively in southern Europe, New Zealand and parts of the USA; its name describes the leaf shape. It is best broadcast on a prepared site at ¼-½oz per yd² (9-17g per m²).

Button weed
Cotula species
A fern-like plant with button-like flowers, best sown broadcast at ¼-½oz per yd² (9-17g per m²). It is not a very dense-growing plant, and a lawn made with it may become infested with the finer grasses.

ALPINE LAWNS

A continuous turf border to the rock garden can be created using a variety of carpet-forming alpine plants together with low-growing herbs such as wild thyme. Useful alpines include species of sedum, arenaria, saxifrage, armeria and dwarf campanulas. It is best to obtain mature plants from a good nursery, and establish them in a bed which has been thoroughly cleared of perennial weeds. The bed need not be level, for such a lawn is not suitable for mowing and should be treated as an extension to the rockery. A few dwarf bulbs and rock outcrops will add interest.

THE SOIL

If the lawn is to thrive it must be made on a well-structured, fertile soil. It is essential to identify the soil type and condition so that it can be improved where necessary, and suitable lawn grasses selected.

FERTILITY AND STRUCTURE

All soils are basically made up of varying amounts of clay, silt, sand and minerals. The texture and structure of each soil type are defined by the proportions of these materials.

The fertility of the soil is a characteristic which only applies to the top layer, known as the topsoil. It is usually a darker colour than the subsoil below, owing to the presence of humus, a dark spongy material created by the breakdown of organic remains by soil bacteria and fungi. Humus contributes to the texture of the soil by joining the individual soil particles into groups, to form the characteristic soil crumb structure. It is also the main natural source of the nutrients required by plants. The subsoil is normally quite lacking in humus.

The acidity of the soil affects plant growth, and it is worth buying a kit to test it. This will enable you to choose the right grasses, and indicate which soil improvers are needed.

CHALKY SOILS

In its natural state a chalky soil is quite dark at the surface, because it consists of a relatively shallow layer of organic topsoil, seldom more than 3in (75mm) thick, overlying a white chalk subsoil. Unless very careful cultivation methods are employed these two layers soon become mixed, and the fertility of the soil is impaired. To correct this, as much organic matter as possible should be introduced, especially green manures such as rape. Some grasses, and all the clovers, do well on chalky soils, and there are seldom drainage problems to cope with.

PEATY SOILS

These soils produce a decidedly acid reaction when tested. Such plants as rhododendron and azalea thrive in them, but many other plants cannot survive. Some of the finer grasses are very tolerant of acid conditions, and do quite well.

The soil at the surface is usually very dark brown or even black, and is generally spongy. Organic matter is present but bacterial life is not plentiful because of the acidity. This impedes the decay of organic matter, and in their natural state such soils are not very fertile. The fertility can be greatly improved by adding lime.

Peat can hold vast amounts of water, and some draining may be necessary.

SANDY SOILS

These soils are generally of quite open texture and free-draining. They normally lack organic matter, and benefit from the incorporation of plenty of well-rotted manure, leafmould or compost. Adding a good balanced fertiliser at the same time will ensure that the young grass gets an adequate initial supply of nitrogen, potash and phosphates. Lawns on such soils always need plenty of feeding, but the finer grasses do particularly well, producing excellent roots in the free-draining soil and giving a really dense surface coverage.

Because of the free-draining nature of such soils irrigation may be necessary in dry weather if the lawn is not to suffer. Drainage problems in wet weather are unusual, but heavy use can cause surface sealing. The cure for this is to break up the surface layers by aeration.

STONY SOILS

Stony soils are usually very free-draining—an asset in winter but a disadvantage in the summer months. Such soils are not easy to work; some of the stones may have to be removed, but it is never good policy to remove them all. Even at the surface only the large stones should be raked out; the small ones should be left to do their job of keeping the soil open, to allow water to drain freely.

As with sandy soils, which have similar characteristics, as much well-rotted manure as possible should be incorporated. The creeping grasses do well on stony land, both on and below the surface.

LOAMS

These are the ideal soils for lawns and gardens in general, for they display all the advantages and very few of the disadvantages of the other soil types. They range from light to heavy in texture; light loams may need additional organic matter, while heavy loams may need draining. The soil crumb structure of the loams is generally good, however, and favours healthy grass growth.

Above: *The topsoil layer is darker than the subsoil below because of its humus content. The two layers should never be mixed, or fertility will be impaired.*

CLAYS

Clay soils are often described as the heavy, or cold soils. Clay is able to retain an enormous volume of water, which increases both its physical weight and the time it takes to warm up in spring. Because of this the clays are always late soils; both vegetable crops and grasses on clay begin to grow relatively late in the season.

A clay soil under drought conditions will crack at the surface because of moisture loss. Conversely it can become upleasantly sticky and slippery during and after heavy rainfall. All the clays are difficult to cultivate, and generally they have a poor soil crumb structure. Good drainage is usually essential, and if fine lawn grasses are to thrive, the texture of the topsoil needs to be improved by the introduction of gritty sand, organic matter and even proprietary soil conditioners, to help break up its natural solidity.

DRAINAGE

Although soil drainage may be simply summarised as 'removing surplus water from the soil' it is a complex subject. Different soils behave in different ways, and to employ the same measures regardless of soil type may lead to trouble.

THE PROBLEM

Ideally, excess water passes down to the lower levels naturally, leaving behind enough to maintain life within the soil. Inadequate drainage may cause waterlogging, which interferes with the availability of oxygen to both plant and animal life. On the other hand, if the soil is too free-draining and dries out, this can also have serious effects, especially on plant life, which depends on the water to carry plant food down through the soil to the root hairs. The balance is critical, and overdraining which occurs either naturally, or as a consequence of man-made drains, can prove just as disastrous as waterlogging.

Light loams, sandy, stony and chalky soils are naturally free-draining, and rarely need artificial help, but the clays and some peaty soils retain large volumes of water and generally require an efficient drainage system if they are to support healthy lawns. A good indication of the need for artificial drainage can be provided by digging some test holes on the site, about 12in (30cm) square and deep, and either filling them to the surface with water or waiting for heavy rainfall to do the same. If the water-level has not gone down appreciably after several hours have elapsed, some form of artificial drainage will be necessary.

Below: *Test holes filled with water will indicate whether the site is free-draining.*

WATER DISPOSAL

When considering any form of drainage the first thing to decide is precisely where the surplus water is to go. An acceptable outlet must be found, and will probably take the form of a soakaway.

The soakaway is aptly named, for it is a collecting area from which the water gradually soaks away well below the surface levels. The natural site is the lowest point of the garden, but it must be chosen with care so as not to burden the neighbours with your excess water. The pit needs to be fairly large, up to 6ft (180cm) square by 8ft (240cm) deep, depending on the subsoil. Having dug out the pit and disposed of the soil, fill the space with stones to within 6in (15cm) of the surface, and cap them with porous soil to prevent puddling at the surface.

TRENCHES AND PIPES

Beneath the lawn the water may be channelled through a network of clay or plastic pipes or rubble-filled trenches, laid or dug with a slight fall in the direction of the soakaway. Bowling greens, golf greens and tennis lawns often require elaborate piped systems, but simple trench drains are usually sufficient for the garden lawn.

A trench drain network normally consists of a main drain dug right across the site and sloping towards the soakaway, with branch drains, or laterals, added on either side at an angle of 45 degrees to the main. The main drain should be about 18-24in (40-60cm) in depth and width. The branch drains should be spaced alternately at 10ft (3m) intervals, and should be 12-18in (30-40cm) in depth and width.

Fill the trenches with large stones for half their depth, followed by smaller stones, broken brick or clinker to within 6in (15cm) of the surface. The topsoil can then be spread back over the top.

A very similar procedure is employed when using pipes. The 4-6in (10-15cm) main drains and 3in (75mm) laterals are placed in the trenches which are then backfilled with porous materials such as gravel or clinker.

Below: *The first requirement of a drainage system is a soakaway (top left) dug deeply into the subsoil and filled with stones. This is fed by the main channel of a herringbone network beneath the lawn (bottom left). Normally trenches filled with stones are sufficient (top right) but pipes set in gravel may be used if needed (bottom right).*

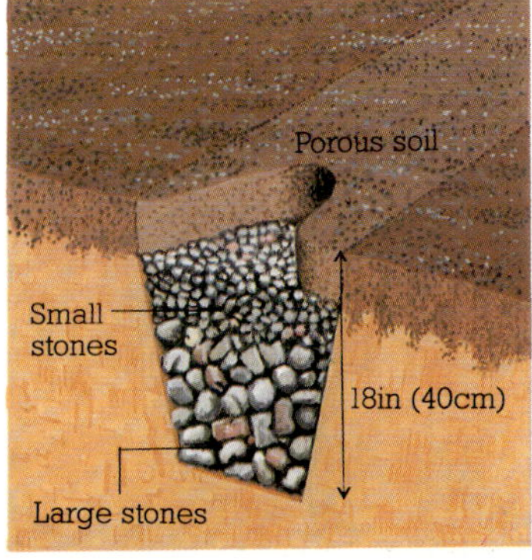

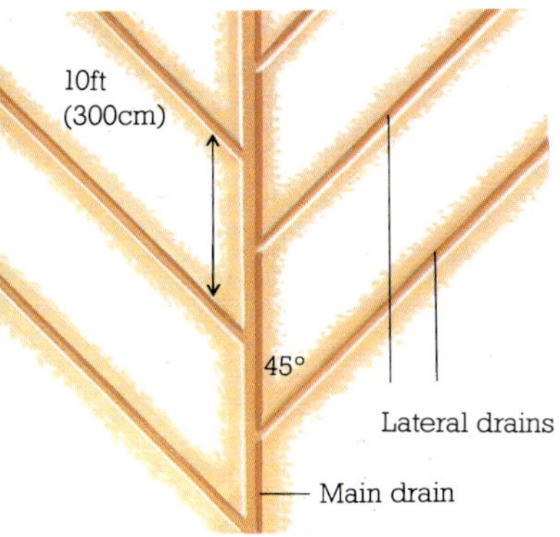

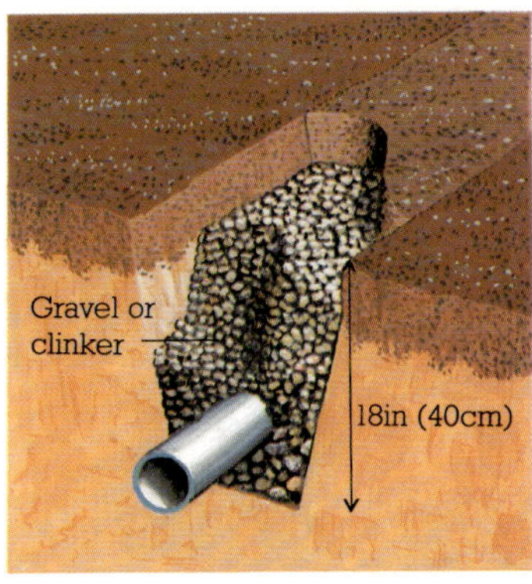

LEVELLING AND LANDSCAPING

It is very unusual to find a site for a lawn that does not need some levelling, and the temptation is to simply scrape the surplus soil off the high spots to fill in the depressions. If you do this you run the risk of removing all the topsoil from one place and doubling its depth in another. The resulting lawn may be level, but it will grow patchily and will never look good.

CONSERVING THE TOPSOIL

The density of the grass blades on the surface of the lawn is roughly proportional to the root development within the soil. If the root system is poor owing to a lack of topsoil the turf will be sparse and open, and liable to infestation by weeds, mosses, lichens and algae. In contrast an extensive root system flourishing in a deep layer of topsoil will cause lush, dense grass growth. Inexpert levelling will create both effects in unsightly patches, and once the work is done there is no simple remedy. Even in the case of very minor levelling care is essential to prevent the loss of topsoil. If true landscaping is undertaken—dealing with appreciable undulations, or perhaps creating terraces on acutely sloping land—drastic measures will be necessary.

If the proposed alteration is going to involve moving more than 3in (75mm) of soil it is essential to begin by removing all the topsoil and stacking it on one side. With the subsoil exposed, you can cut and fill as much as you want. When you have achieved a flat surface—or whatever landscape effect you have been aiming at—you can replace the topsoil in an even layer. You should have at least 6in (15cm) of fertile topsoil for really healthy grass development. If there is not enough, buy an extra load or two from a local supplier.

LEVELLING TECHNIQUE

Levelling, both before and after replacing the topsoil, can be carried out using a supply of wooden pegs and a straight plank about 10ft (3m) long, with a spirit level attached midway along

Below: *Crude levelling of a bumpy site (top) will result in uneven topsoil depth (centre). To prevent this remove all topsoil before levelling, and replace it in an even layer (bottom).*

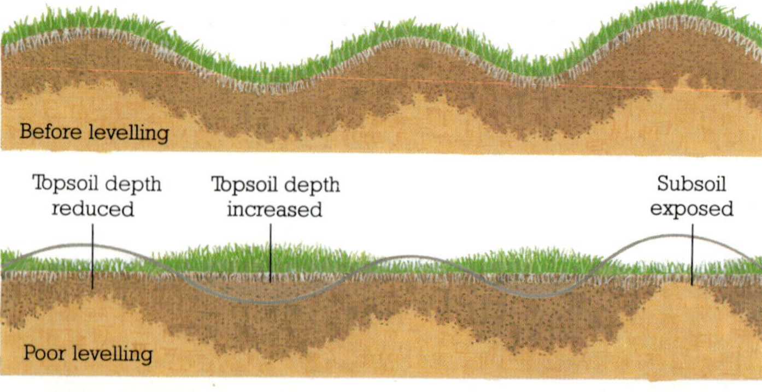

one face. Cut the pegs from 1in (25mm) square timber; they should be about 8in (20cm) long. Mark a line 3in (75mm) from the top of each peg.

Choosing a dry day, start levelling from the centre of the site, driving in the first, master peg until the indicator line is level with the surface. Space out the other pegs at roughly 8ft (240cm) intervals, and tap them gently into the surface. Then, working outwards from the master peg, adjust the soil and the pegs until all the pegs are at the same height—using the plank and spirit level as a reference—and the indicator lines on every peg are level with the surface. As the work goes on tread the surface thoroughly to ensure it is properly firmed down. This will help prevent settlement later on.

Above: *Level the site using wooden pegs, a straight plank and a spirit level, moving soil until the ground surface is parallel with the level plank.*

This work should be carried out well in advance of seedbed preparation, so that a final critical levelling can be done to correct the effects of high winds or heavy rainfall. The pegs should only be taken out when you are ready to sow the seed or lay the turf.

SEEDING AND TURFING

Even if there is no major levelling or landscaping to be done, the lawn site will still need proper cultivation before sowing the grass seed or laying the turf. Both methods demand the same degree of preparation if the lawn is to succeed.

CULTIVATION

Dig over the site to the depth of a spade, removing all weed roots, stems and other plant debris, and any builders' rubbish such as broken bricks, concrete and pieces of wire and timber. Where trees and shrubs have been disposed of, make sure that the entire root system has been taken out. Avoid making fires of rubbish on the lawn site; the effects will be visible in the grass for months afterwards.

Using an ordinary garden rake, break up the clods and generally level up the site. Rake out and remove all large stones—over 2in (50mm) in diameter—in the top 6in (15cm) of soil, but leave the smaller stones to assist the natural drainage.

Before starting to create the final surface, take a critical look at the topsoil. For grass the soil should be firm, but not compacted; it may be necessary to add extra organic matter to improve the texture. Really well-rotted farmyard manure can be forked in at a rate of 1yd^3 per 100yd^2 (1m^3 per 100m^2). Do not use fresh farmyard or poultry manure as this may inhibit seed germination or turf establishment. Properly processed town waste or sewerage is sometimes available in powder form, and safe to use at a rate of about 4lb per yd^2 (2kg per m^2). Fine grade peat, applied at 2lb per yd^2 (1kg per m^2), will improve sandy soils or light loams.

It is always wise to incorporate a good balanced lawn fertiliser about a week before sowing or turfing, to ensure a proper supply of the basic plant foods and to get the grass off to a good start. Once the grass is growing it is better not to risk applying further fertiliser dressings until the lawn is about six months old, or the grass may be scorched.

Anything added to the topsoil must be evenly spread and thoroughly incorporated, to avoid creating pockets of high or low fertility which will eventually influence grass growth.

PREPARING THE SURFACE

Well-shod feet and a good rake are more effective than any machine for producing the firm, friable surface ideal for turf or grass seed. The area needs

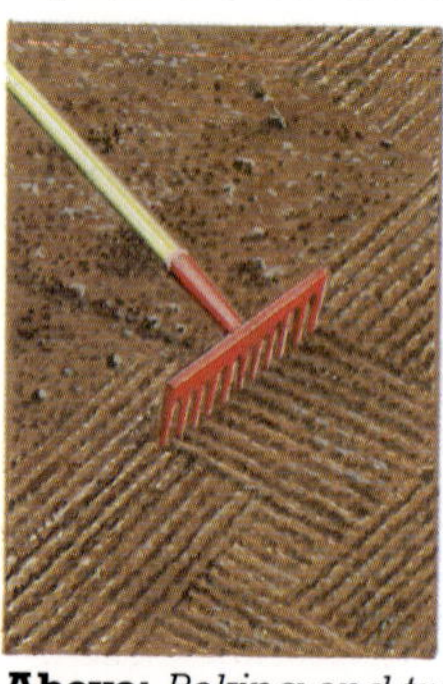

Above: *Raking and treading is the best way to prepare the lawn site. After treading all over the soil should be raked across the direction of treading to fill any depressions (left). Repeat until treading leaves only shallow prints (centre). A roller (right) can be used, but will not be so effective.*

Above: *The soil on the raked and trodden site should be airy but firm, with no pockets of soft earth which could form hollows in the lawn. Kill any weeds using a hoe.*

treading all over in one direction, using a heel-and-toe action, and then lightly raking at right angles to the direction of treading. After this, tread again in the direction of the raking and rake again at right angles. These operations are essential to the ultimate success of the lawn, and may need doing as many as six times each. When walking on the surface leaves only a slight imprint of your heel and toe you will have achieved perfection, and a final gentle raking will produce the seed or turf bed.

If the area is too large for the treading and raking treatment you can use a roller—provided it weighs less than 3cwt (150kg). Draw the roller very slowly over the site, rake as before and repeat, changing direction each time the whole area has been covered.

SEEDING

If the lawn is to be seeded it is important to choose a mixture that is well suited to the site, soil type and conditions, as well as the final purpose of the lawn. A very shady area is best sown with a "shady site" mixture, which will probably contain a high proportion of rough-stalked meadowgrass. A chalky soil or a very sandy soil may demand the use of a special blend—in any event check that the mixture you buy will thrive on such a soil. Finally, do not sow a high-quality blend of fine-bladed grasses intended for ornamental use when you know that the lawn will get hard wear. Use a utility

Above top: *A balanced fertiliser applied no later than a week before sowing will ensure that the grass gets a good start. Even distribution is vital.*

Above left: *The seed needs to be securely anchored in the soil or it may be blown away or washed out by heavy rain. Light rolling may help on some soils.*

mixture, probably one which contains ryegrass.

The seed should be evenly sown at a rate of 1-2oz per yd² (34-68g per m²), into shallow furrows produced by gentle raking of the seedbed. If the sowing rate is too low the new lawn will be very sparse, and if it is too heavy the thickly-growing seedlings may be killed by damping-off disease. 1½oz per yd² (53g per m²) is usually sufficient, unless seed-eating birds are particularly active. It is best to calculate the area and weigh off the amount needed for the whole lawn. Then divide the seed into two equal batches and broadcast one batch over the whole area, working from one end of the site. Sow the second batch from one side, at right angles to the first. Alternatively the lawn area can be divided into yard (or metre) squares using strings and pegs, before sowing the correct weight of seed in each, half one way across the square and half the other. Either method will ensure even coverage.

Cover the seed by light cross-raking, and protect it from birds using scarers or a network of black threads stretched between sticks pushed into the soil at the edge of the site. The seedlings

Above: *Within a few weeks of sowing, if the weather is kind, the new lawn will be ready for the first cut which will thicken up the grass.*

should begin to show within seven to ten days.

The grass should be trimmed for the first time when the seedling plants are about 3in (75mm) tall. Use a sharp-bladed machine, set to cut off about 1in (25mm) of growth—no more. This will make the plants "tiller", or thicken out at the base and produce additional leaves.

Mow the grass regularly after this, gradually reducing the standing height of the plants to 1in (25mm). During the first year of growth the lawn should be cut not closer than ½in (13mm)—indeed this is the ideal final height for an all-purpose lawn.

WEEDS AND PESTS

If your soil is really fertile, it is almost inevitable that some weeds will make their appearance at the same time as the grass. Do not be surprised if some of the weeds are unfamiliar; the natural reaction is to blame the grass seed, but in fact the weeds will have sprouted from disturbed seeds which may have lain dormant in the soil for many years.

One way to deal with these is to allow a fallow period—the unseeded, prepared land is left for a few weeks to allow the weeds to come through. They can then be killed using a general, quick-acting weedkiller such as paraquat, which will allow the grass seed to be sown a few days later.

Once the lawn is properly

established you will have to use selective weedkiller, or weed by hand. It is not safe to use selective weedkillers until you have been able to mow the lawn six or seven times; by then the root system should be robust and deep enough to prevent the absorption of any chemical which reaches the soil surface.

When large weeds are pulled out by hand always put down a plank to tread on. Cover the area round the weed with your flattened hand, and pull it through your fingers; this helps prevent the lawn surface from being torn up with the weed.

Wormcasts on the new lawn can be a nuisance. Left on the surface they may be flattened, and could kill the grass. They can be dispersed with a whippy bamboo cane or stiff brush when they are dry.

Keep watch for any small irregularly-shaped brown or reddish areas. These could indicate one of the many forms of damping-off disease which attack all manner of seedlings, including grasses. The disease spreads rapidly, so very prompt treatment is essential.

Pale yellow patches could indicate the effects of animal urine, or stones or subsoil near the surface.

Most companies treat grass seed to make it distasteful to birds without causing them—or any other living things—any harm. Remember however that treated seed will not physically keep the birds off; they have to sample the seed to discover the unpleasant taste, and you may lose quite a lot in the process. Bird scarers are often more effective.

You may wish to water the new lawn to encourage germination, but do not start such a campaign if you will be unable to keep it up. You will need to use about 1½ gallons per yd² (7 litres per m²) every other day at least—that is a lot of water, even if you use a sprinkler.

Above: *If the grass seed fails (top) it may be necessary to clear the site with a general weedkiller and start again. Even if germination is good (above) there will be many weeds to deal with, but they are usually easy to remove by hand.*
Below: *When weeding the new lawn, keep surface damage to a minimum by holding down the surrounding soil and pulling up the weed between your fingers.*

TURFING

Turf should be chosen with care. Fortunately you no longer have to rely on worn-out agricultural turf "doctored" to look good. There are now specialist growers who produce excellent turf composed of proper lawn grasses. Before buying, try to secure a sample, or better still, visit the source and see the turf before it is lifted.

Turfing is more expensive than seeding, but it does give you an attractive lawn in a shorter time. The pieces of turf should be supplied cut to a standard size and uniform thickness, ready for laying when the grasses are making root growth in autumn, winter and early spring. Lay them on the prepared surface in a brickwork pattern, to avoid too many long joints. You will need a supply of clean, fertile sifted soil—about 2lb per yd^2

Above: *Using turf, a lawn can be created in a few hours, but it will not be fit for hard wear for many weeks. The separate pieces of turf must be given time to knit together, and root into the soil beneath.*
Below: *The turf is laid in staggered rows so that four joints never meet. Laying the turf round the corner as shown avoids using small pieces to fill gaps at the edge of the lawn.*

(1kg per m²)—to brush into the joints when the job is complete.

If the surface is dry the turf can be rolled to ensure that the pieces knit together properly and stay in contact with the soil, to encourage new root growth. Assuming the turf is weed-free when supplied, and that you have properly cleaned and prepared the site, there should be no immediate weed problems.

Keep off the newly-turfed area in frosty conditions, or you may cause irreparable damage to the grass. Turf can be lifted by really heavy frost, but resettlement by rolling should only be attempted when the ground is thoroughly thawed out.

Above top: *Before laying turf rake the soil beneath to level it and open it up, so that the grass roots can penetrate. If the turf thickness is uneven, contour the soil to fit.*

Above: *As you lay the turf, check that the grasses are healthy and making good root growth, and pull out any weeds. Press each piece hard against the others to reduce gaps.*

Do not be tempted to mow the grass too closely in the early stages. Give it time to acclimatise after the root pruning caused by the cutting and lifting process, and the total change of environment. The hover mower is ideal, as it exerts the minimum pressure and cuts cleanly if the grass is not completely dry.

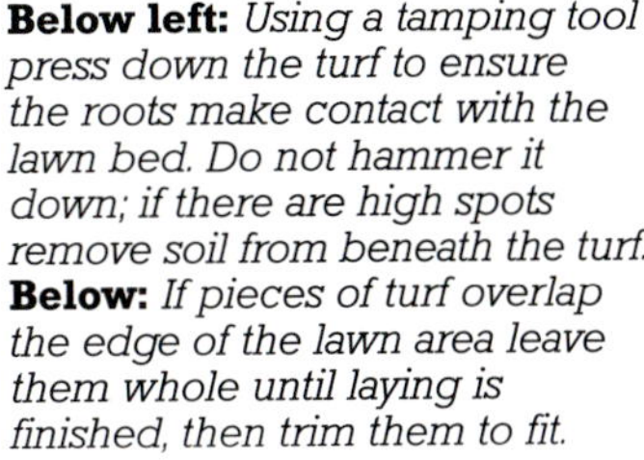

Below left: *Using a tamping tool press down the turf to ensure the roots make contact with the lawn bed. Do not hammer it down; if there are high spots remove soil from beneath the turf.*
Below: *If pieces of turf overlap the edge of the lawn area leave them whole until laying is finished, then trim them to fit.*

Above: *After tamping down the turf, fill any small holes with compost mixed with a little grass seed. Brush compost into the joints to encourage the turf to knit together.*

Above: *Trim the edge of the turfed lawn using an edging iron against a guide. If necessary create a gully between the lawn and nearby walls or paving to allow the edge to be trimmed.*

Maintenance

Maintaining a lawn in good condition involves a lot more than occasional cutting with a mower. The edges have to be kept in order, weeds kept in check, and pests and diseases discouraged. The grass should be fed, and sometimes watered, and the turf kept healthy by regular aeration. The work does not take long, and may save drastic renovation measures later on.

MOWING

Although mowing is essential to the maintenance of turf, poor mowing can do more harm to the grass than almost anything else. Many people mow their lawns far too short, either because they think they want the grass no higher than the thickness of the felt on a billiard table, or because they believe that close cropping will save mowing the lawn too often. The resulting drastic defoliation interferes with all the normal processes of the plant. It cuts down respiration, the intake of carbon and manufacture of food within the leaves, and reduces moisture loss from the foliage which in turn reduces the absorption of water and nutrients through the roots. The grass is severely weakened, and may die.

HOW MUCH AND WHEN?

Really beautiful lawns are never cut too closely; the height of the grass is maintained by mowing frequently, and at regular intervals. In this way the grass is never subjected to really severe cropping, even though the height of the foliage is kept quite short.

Some of the finest mixtures of grasses used for ornamental lawns produce turf which can be left unmown for up to three weeks, but the coarser grasses used for utility lawns grow much faster. The average lawn needs cutting at least once a week, and some may require more frequent mowing at the height of the season.

During spring and summer ornamental lawns look their best, and grow well, when regularly cut to a height of ¼-½in (6-13mm). Utility lawns, especially the children's play areas, do better when they are maintained at ½-1in (13-25mm). It is good policy to continue mowing as long as the grass continues to grow—and in some areas the grass makes top growth throughout the year, sometimes at the expense of root development. The height of the cut should be raised during the autumn, winter and early spring, and if the spring and summer minimum is ¼-½in (6-13mm), then in autumn, winter and early spring the cut should be raised to about ¾in (19mm). Never let the lawn retain a shaggy unkempt appearance when a "topping" could put matters right. Grass which grows long during the winter can cause problems in the spring.

WHICH MOWER?

For general use, on a luxury lawn, a cylinder mower with a roller is considered to give the best results—but the machine has to be perfectly adjusted and the blades quite sharp, otherwise the effect will be disappointing, to say the least.

Make sure the mower has at least five blades and preferably more; if there are too few blades the machine will tend to create a ribbed effect where bands of grass have escaped cutting. If this occurs, try to vary the direction of the mowing as often as possible, so that each mowing counteracts the effect of the one before.

A rotary mower or a hover mower is an excellent choice for an all-purpose lawn. Both use the principle of a horizontally-rotating scythe blade, which only requires height adjustment to be efficient. Easy to maintain, they can be used in conditions that would defeat a cylinder mower; autumn and winter mowing, for example, is much easier if you use a hover mower, since the surface is seldom really dry enough for a cylinder type to be used effectively without risking damage to the grass.

Below: *The striped effect often favoured for ornamental lawns can be created by careful brushing or rolling, but it is normally achieved using a mower fitted with a back roller.*

Above: *A hover mower is easy to use in a tight situation, and is a good choice for a landscaped or irregularly-shaped lawn.*

PREPARATION

Before starting to mow, make sure the machine is running freely, and that the blades are sharp and properly adjusted. Blunt blades (or cylinder blades that do not meet) will chew the grass rather than cutting it cleanly, and the bruised foliage is an ideal breeding ground for diseases. Check the cutting height on both sides, and ensure that the bottom blade of a cylinder mower is not distorted.

If you are using a petrol mower, make sure that there are no petrol or oil leaks which could result in dead patches of grass. Fill the petrol tank before you start, while the mower is off the lawn.

Try to mow when there is no dew or rainwater on the grass. Although many machines can mow quite adequately when the foliage is wet—particularly rotary and hover mowers—it is generally agreed that the very best results are secured only when the grass is quite dry. Check on the condition of the soil as well. Even if the grass appears to be dry the soil may be waterlogged, and mowing with any machine other than a hover mower may churn up the turf.

Ensure that the lawn is free of small obstructions; the odd stone or bottle top, or a stray bolt from a child's tricycle or scooter can cause havoc to the machine and may injure the user or a bystander if it is thrown out. Do a little tour of inspection —it will not be time wasted. If there are wormcasts on the lawn, scatter them with a brush, otherwise the mower—particularly one fitted with a roller—will flatten them.

DURING MOWING

If you want to create the striped effect, using a mower fitted with a roller, you will have to give some thought to the mowing sequence. The pattern on the grass will reflect the final pass of the mower over the area, so cut all the awkward places first, before mowing the main part of the lawn in a regular up-and-down sequence. With a simple rectangular lawn, mow across each end before starting on the main area, and the lengthwise stripes will erase the transverse stripes at the ends. If you finish on the far side of the lawn, bring the mower back by running it down the edge, so as not to disrupt the pattern.

It is a good idea to alter the direction of mowing every time, particularly if your mower tends to leave ridges. Do not become so attached to your stripe pattern that you cannot change it.

Hover mowers and rotaries without rollers will not make stripes, and the precise direction of mowing is not so critical. Nevertheless it is still best to work methodically, so as not to waste power and effort mowing the same area twice.

Above: *Collecting the grass clippings helps to reduce lawn thatch. The Nutrivac system fitted to some hover mowers uses the hover fan to suck the clippings off the lawn surface.*

Always use the grass collection box, if the mower is fitted with one. There are some advantages in leaving clippings on the lawn—nutrients are returned to the soil and water loss during dry weather is reduced—but if all the clippings are returned each time you mow there is risk of encouraging worm activity, disease and weeds. A thick thatch of debris will also impede aeration. Many mowers now have very large-capacity grass-boxes, cutting down the emptying time, and some also shred the clippings to encourage quick decay in the compost heap.

TAKE CARE!

- Always wear a stout pair of shoes while mowing, and keep your feet well away from the blades.
- Never make any adjustments to a power mower without first disconnecting the power supply or spark plug lead.
- When using a mains electric mower, keep the cable away from the blades. Start on the side nearest the power point, moving steadily away so that there is no risk of overrunning the cable.
- While mowing, keep children and pets off the lawn.

EDGING

The finest turf will look untidy and badly maintained if the edges are not kept in good order. Careful design can provide an edge that will stay neat without attention, but in most cases special edging techniques have to be used.

DESIGN

Many of the difficulties associated with making a neat edge to the lawn can be avoided by good design. For example, taking the lawn right up against a brick or stone wall creates a problem; the lawnmower cannot get close enough to cut the grass, which then grows too long and spoils the appearance of both the lawn and the wall. It can only be cut laboriously by hand, or using a nylon-line trimmer. By laying a strip of paving at the foot of the wall, on a level slightly below that of the grass, the problem is eliminated. The mower can be used with one wheel on the grass and the other on the paving, and the lawn edge will take care of itself. The same principle can be used for paths and adjoining patios, or to provide a decorative stone or brick surround for the lawn area.

EDGING TECHNIQUES

If the boundaries of the lawn are not contained by paving, you will have to keep the edges in order with an edging tool. There are many different types available. The simplest, ideal for the small to medium sized lawn, is a pair of long-handled shears designed to trim the edge by neatly cutting off the surplus foliage. If they are well set and sharp they are quick and easy to use, and employed

Above: *Edging shears are an essential tool for every lawn owner. Used regularly, they are very quick and efficient.*
Right: *Neglected edges will need trimming with an edging iron. A plank acts as a guide for a straight cut, while garden hose will give a smooth curve.*

regularly, at every mowing, they are very effective.

For a larger lawn it is worth considering one of the mechanical edgers. These use revolving blades to do a similar job, but they usually demand a reasonably tidy edge to start with. Some are designed for vertical cutting only, while others can be used for both vertical and horizontal cutting.

An edge that has been neglected, or has crumbled or broken, will need recutting. This can be done with a garden spade, but it is far better to use a proper half-moon edging iron, which will make a clean, straight, vertical cut—unlike a spade which, being dished, produces a scalloped effect. If you have a good eye the edging iron may be used freehand, but for the best results it is advisable to use a guide. Use a long plank or a tightly-stretched line for a straight cut, and a garden hose as a guide for a smooth curve. Remember that frequent edging using this method will soon reduce the area of the lawn.

EDGE REINFORCEMENT

Burred and broken lawn edges can be prevented by using metal or plastic edging strips. Inserted next to the natural lawn edge, slightly below the level of the surface, they need not be at all unsightly; they may not even show. For the busy gardener they are an extremely useful aid to keeping the lawn tidy and maintaining a well-kept appearance.

Below: *A brick edge to the lawn can be very attractive and allows the grass edge to be kept neat using only the mower.*

FEEDING THE LAWN

Few gardeners would expect to grow fine vegetables or flowers without using fertilisers or manures, yet many lawn owners assume that grass is self-sufficient. In fact, once the fertilisers incorporated when making the lawn have been used up, the grass will need regular feeding to stay in good condition.

FOOD SOURCES

Like all green plants grass is able to absorb carbon from the air and combine it with water, using energy from sunlight, to make sugars. The process—photosynthesis—is a major source of plant foods, but by itself it is not enough. Raw materials must also be obtained from the soil through the root hairs, to be converted into plant foods within the foliage.

Some of these substances are needed in quite large quantities, and form a major part of most manures and fertilisers. Others are required in comparatively small amounts, but they are still essential to plant health. These "trace elements" are often naturally present in the soil and in organic manures, and are normally left out of ordinary artificial fertilisers.

Below: *A calibrated fertiliser distributor ensures even application, and prevents any scorching of the grass foliage.*

MAJOR NUTRIENTS

The most important plant nutrients are nitrogen, phosphorous and potash. Wild grasses obtain nitrogen from decaying organic matter in the soil; any garden soil which is low in organic matter will be low in nitrogen, and the grass will grow slowly and lose colour.

Phosphorous and potash are found in soil minerals as well as organic matter. Phosphorous is essential to healthy root growth, but it should be used sparingly on the lawn as it encourages the clovers at the expense of the grasses. Potash helps to produce the fruits and seeds of most plants, but on the lawn it keeps the grass healthy and green.

TRACE ELEMENTS

Of the many minor nutrients needed to ensure complete grass health the most important are manganese, copper, boron, molybdenum and iron. A deficiency of manganese causes

MAJOR NUTRIENTS

NITROGEN	
For foliage growth and colour	
Ammonium Sulphate 21% Nitrogen ½oz per yd^2 17g per m^2 Apply mixed with sand or compost, or in water	**Dried Blood** 12-13% Nitrogen 1oz per yd^2 34g per m^2 Apply dry
Hoof and Horn Meal 12-13% Nitrogen 2oz per yd^2 68g per m^2 Apply dry	**Urea** 38% Nitrogen 1-2oz per yd^2 34-68g per m^2 Apply dissolved in water
Also an ingredient of fertiliser mixtures	

PHOSPHOROUS	
For healthy root development	
Superphosphate of Lime 16-21% Phosphate ½oz per yd^2 17g per m^2 May be dissolved in water for application	**Bone Meal** 20-30% Phosphate 1oz per yd^2 34g per m^2 Insoluble; apply dry Slow-release effect
Also an ingredient of fertiliser mixtures	

POTASH	
For grass health and good colour	
Sulphate of Potash 50% Potash ½-1oz per yd^2 17-34g per m^2 Apply mixed with sand or compost	**Muriate of Potash** 60% Potash ½-1oz per yd^2 17-34g per m^2 Apply mixed with sand or compost
Also an ingredient of fertiliser mixtures	

a lack of chlorophyll, the green material which absorbs the sunlight needed for photosynthesis. New peaty and sandy soils may lack copper, causing poor growth, and old acid soils may have a boron deficiency. Iron plays a part in disease resistance, and it is often included in lawn fertiliser mixtures.

FERTILISER MIXTURES

Most lawn fertilisers are mixtures of the major nutrients, and some contain trace elements. Many are clearly labelled as NPK fertilisers, N, P and K being the scientific abbreviations for nitrogen, phosphorous and potassium. The proportions of the mixtures vary; fertilisers intended for spring application may contain extra nitrogen to encourage leaf growth, whereas mixtures for autumn use contain more phosphorous to promote root development. Some of the more complex mixtures, known as compound fertilisers, have both fast-acting and slow-acting ingredients. They are more expensive, but the effects last longer.

APPLICATION

Lawn fertilisers are normally applied as powders or small granules, particularly those with slow-release ingredients which are insoluble in water. Simple spreaders are available which ensure even distribution.

It is important to avoid using dry fertilisers during a drought; most types need to be washed off the foliage into the soil, or they will cause chemical scorching of the leaves. Unless rain falls within about 48 hours of application it is a sensible precaution to water the dressing into the lawn.

Liquid fertilisers are gaining in popularity. The active ingredients are dissolved in water, and they can be applied through the watering system using special diluting attachments. Unfortunately the insoluble slow-release types are not suited to this technique, but some of the trace elements are most effective when applied in liquid form. Instead of going into the soil they enter the plant through the leaf pores, and are rapidly absorbed into the plant system.

Always follow the manufacturer's instructions when using either solid or liquid fertilisers, and pay particular attention to both the recommended rate and frequency of application. With some of the more complex compound fertilisers, one

Below: *Never mix top dressing on the lawn. Prepare the mixture under cover, then take it to the site on a dry day and spread it evenly in yard-wide strips along and across the lawn.*

application may be enough for a whole season's growth.

TOP DRESSING WITH COMPOST

Although chemical fertilisers can supply the nutrients which the lawn grasses need, they do not improve the texture of the soil in the same way as organic manures. Golf course greenkeepers have always appreciated the value of compost. Many make huge compost heaps, allowing the material to mature for three years before spreading it on the greens as a top dressing, usually after aeration by mechanical tining has reduced compaction problems.

In the average garden the compost—often made with grass cuttings—is usually reserved for the vegetable plots or the flower beds, and not the lawn. It is often necessary to make up a top dressing with similar properties, using soil and peat. A good mixture for annual use consists of four parts sterilised loamy soil (by volume), one part fine grade peat, and five parts washed, sharp gritty sand, thoroughly blended together.

Spread the dressing on the lawn, after aeration, to an even depth of just over ⅛in (3mm), then work it into the aeration holes using the back of a rake, or one of the special implements available for the purpose. The top dressing is best applied in autumn, so that it does not interfere with mowing.

Below: *Spread the top dressing to an even depth of about ⅛in (3mm). Work it into the turf with the back of a rake, or use an old footscraper. Brush off the excess with a stiff brush.*

IRRIGATION

Careful attention to the seed mixture will produce a lawn which will tolerate long periods without rain, but even the strongest grasses will need water eventually. Irrigation may be necessary if the turf is to survive.

Above: *An oscillating sprinkler is ideal for a rectangular lawn.*
Below: *The static sprinkler is simple and very efficient.*

WHY THE GRASS NEEDS WATER

Water is essential to all plants, and soil moisture is particularly valuable since it contains dissolved plant nutrients. In healthy topsoil, each crumb of soil has some moisture locked within the particles, which will only evaporate under intense heat. Normally, there is also a film of water covering the surface of each soil crumb, and a droplet of moisture at the base.

The soil moisture, with its dissolved nutrients, is taken in by the roots as the plants transpire from the leaf pores; the moisture given off at the leaves evaporates into the atmosphere, forms clouds, and eventually falls back to earth as rain. Under ideal climatic conditions the soil moisture used up by the plants would always be replaced by rainfall, but unfortunately normal weather patterns are far from ideal. During prolonged dry periods the soil loses a great deal of water by plant transpiration and direct evaporation. Eventually, if the dry spell persists, nearly all the soil moisture is used up, and there is not enough to dissolve the plant nutrients and carry them into the roots. If grass plants succumb under drought conditions they do not die of thirst, but of starvation.

WATERING TACTICS

When there is not enough rain to keep the soil moist, irrigation will ensure continued transpiration and food intake by the grass plants. Unfortunately the shortage of drinking water which usually occurs during a prolonged drought often leads to restrictions on the use of hosepipes and lawn sprinklers.

At such times the value of using a proper blend of tufted and creeping grasses in the lawn becomes evident. The tufted grasses may fail, but the creeping grasses have a high capacity for survival, being able to store

Below: *Rotary sprinklers (top) give greater coverage than the static type, but pulse-jet models (bottom) are the most powerful.*

food in their stolons and rhizomes. The foliage of such grasses may die back, but when rain falls again the plants sprout new leaves and the lawn quickly revives.

The lawn will often benefit from irrigation well before the drought becomes severe enough for restrictions to be imposed. How much, and how often, depends on the precise condition and composition of the soil beneath the turf. If a layer of fibre (old undecomposed dead roots) has accumulated, this may have forced the living roots to remain very close to the surface, and the grass plants will suffer unless they are watered very frequently indeed—perhaps every other day. This will certainly be necessary if the porous layer has dried out, since it will then act rather like a sponge, absorbing and holding all the water you apply until it is saturated.

As a general guide, you should try to water the lawn at least twice a week during a dry spell. The work should be done in the late evening to ensure minimal loss from evaporation.

Never apply less than the equivalent of ¼in (6mm) of rainfall; to allow for normal loss by evaporation this will mean using about 1¼ gallons per yd^2 (6·5 litres per m^2). Use as fine a spray as possible to simulate gentle rainfall rather than a sudden cloudburst; never flood the surface: move the sprinkler around as often as possible to prevent puddles forming.

There are many types of sprinkler available for use on lawns, ranging from the electrically-operated pop-up types used on golf courses, and self-propelled miniature tractors which follow a pattern of laid-out hose, to relatively simple sprinklers which fit on to the end of the garden hose and water a small area at a time. A reasonable water pressure of about 30lb per in^2 (2kg per cm^2) is necessary to operate these devices.

Tap water is never as good for grass as rainwater, which invariably contains trace elements which make a valuable contribution to plant health. Nevertheless most domestic supply water is perfectly safe for use on lawns, although in some areas where the chalk content is high it may cause temporary discoloration of the foliage.

AERATION

To grow well, all plants including grass need an ample supply of air to the roots. The soil around individual plants in the rest of the garden can be cultivated to loosen it and let in air, but this is not practicable on the lawn, and special aeration techniques are needed.

THE NATURAL WAY

Natural aeration of the soil is carried out by the creatures that inhabit the upper layer, or topsoil. As they move around in search of food they create tunnels which act as air ducts, aerating the soil beneath the densest turf or undergrowth.

The most important of these creatures is the earthworm, which not only aerates the topsoil but improves its fertility and texture. Unfortunately for the lawnowner, some species dump the improved soil on the surface as wormcasts, which can smother the grass if left to be flattened underfoot. In severe cases the worms may have to be sacrificed to keep the turf healthy. This makes artificial methods of aeration essential.

BRUSHING AND RAKING

The surface of the soil can be broken up with a stiff brush or rake, without damaging the grass plants unduly. Brushing is less effective, but may be more appropriate with a fairly new lawn. Raking is more drastic; it not only disturbs the soil but also removes the old plant debris. This is most beneficial, particularly if it is done in the autumn. If the lawn has acquired a thick layer of debris, or lawn thatch, hard raking will open it up, let the air in, and give the grass a new lease of life.

If the lawn is too big for hand raking, which can be very tiring, mechanised scarifiers are available which do the same job.

Brushing and raking will break

Above: *Raking teases out plant debris and opens up the surface, allowing air to circulate round the plant roots.*

Above: *The tines of a fork make deep air channels, but they may be compacted at the sides.*

Above: *Hollow tining removes cores of soil, improving aeration without causing compaction.*

Above: *Hand aeration is hard work. Machine tining, using solid or hollow tines, is just as effective and much quicker.*

Above: *Gently sweeping up the debris with a brush after hollow tining will tone up the whole lawn surface.*

up the surface, but for thorough aeration, essential when the soil is compacted by hard use, you will need an implement capable of penetrating deep into the ground to introduce air into the soil around and beneath the plant roots.

The simplest technique is to use the garden fork, driving the tines straight in and out at regular intervals. Air will penetrate the vertical channels and the plants will be encouraged to extend their roots into the spaces. Obviously such piercing is a slow process using an ordinary fork, but there are machines available which work on the same principle, and make the job much less time-consuming.

Lawn grasses renew their roots in the autumn and early winter, and in a properly aerated soil with ample bacterial activity the old roots decay and are converted into humus, which in turn helps to feed the grass plants. This process can be encouraged by using an aerating machine fitted with slitting tines, which have sharp edges designed to cut through both the soil and the grass roots. The grass responds by growing more roots, so the treatment serves the dual purpose of letting air in and encouraging more active root development.

A refinement of this principle is the hollow tine, which removes a core of soil and deposits it on the surface. Excellent aeration and root pruning are achieved, and the holes can be filled with manure or compost to encourage bacterial life and organically improve the soil. This will also improve the water retention of very free-draining light land.

If the surface drainage is poor, fine grade charcoal can be introduced; this will sweeten the soil and dispel the effects of stagnation. Sharp gritty sand can also be worked in to assist water percolation through heavy clay soils.

The ejected cores left on the lawn surface after hollow tining should be swept off and added to the compost heap—they are certainly much too rich in plant food to be wasted.

REPAIRS AND RENOVATION

Many lawns are marred by bumps and hollows, broken edges, stagnant areas caused by poor drainage, and patches of weed. A few simple repairs will often effect a vast improvement in appearance.

BUMPS AND HOLLOWS

An uneven surface is not very attractive, and is very likely to be damaged during mowing. While the grass in a hollow grows longer than it should, high areas may be scalped; in extreme cases the grass may be sliced off to expose the soil beneath.

Shallow depressions can be built up by selective top-dressing with soil, compost or a mixture of soil, sand and peat. The grass must not be buried, or it will die, so use relatively light dressings of about 6lb per yd^2 (3kg per m^2). As each dressing is applied to the low area, work it in carefully using the back of a garden rake, a drag mat or an implement designed for the purpose. As soon as the grass has grown through, apply another layer. Repeat the process until the sunken area has been raised to the level of the rest of the lawn.

Below: *Patches of lush grass may indicate surface hollows or may be caused by an uneven thickness of topsoil created by crude levelling or earlier repairs.*

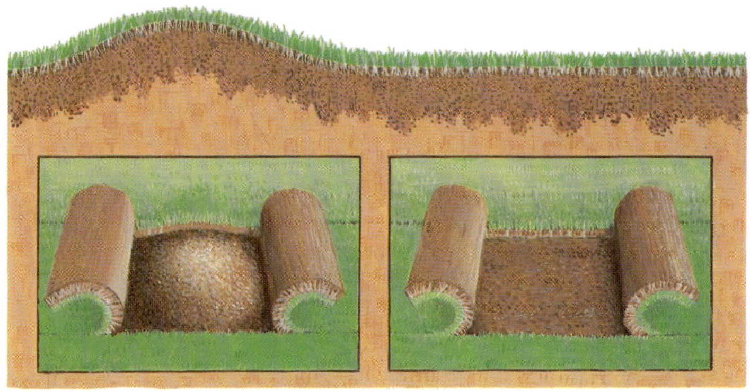

Above: *To correct a bump in the lawn, simply cut across the highest part, slice the turf away from the soil beneath and roll it away (left). Remove the surplus soil (right), roll the turf back and press down firmly. If the topsoil layer is shallow (top) remove the surplus from the subsoil beneath.*

Above: *To fill a hollow, spread compost or clean soil on the surface and work it in well.*

Above: *After removing a large weed, fill the hole with compost or clean soil mixed with a little grass seed.*

It is surprisingly easy to create a flat surface on a naturally bumpy lawn, simply by paying proper attention to regular top-dressing. The treatment is best carried out in spring, autumn or even winter, when the grass is making root growth rather than leaf growth. Any dressings given in late spring or summer can be a nuisance during mowing, and will soon blunt the machine. All dressings should be worked well into the sward, and if some form of aeration can be carried out beforehand, so much the better.

Deeper hollows or raised areas need more drastic treatment, but they can be dealt with quite quickly. Using a half-moon edging iron, cut a letter H in the turf to a depth of 1½in (40mm), with the bar of the H crossing the middle of the faulty area. Sever the roots under the turf with a spade or turfing iron, and roll back the turf in both directions to expose the soil below.

If the area is too high, simply remove the excess soil. If it is too low, build it up with good loamy soil or potting compost. Then replace the turf, cutting out any surplus at the centre, and tread it down firmly.

Above: *Local edge damage is easily repaired by cutting round and beneath the area (left) to form a separate turf. This can then be turned round to make a new edge (right). Fill the hole with potting compost or clean soil and reseed it.*

BROKEN EDGES

Edge damage should be repaired as quickly as possible before it gets worse. Building up a new edge is difficult, so cut out the square or rectangle of turf which includes the broken edge and reverse it. This creates a new, strong edge, and converts the damaged area into a hole which can be filled with soil and compost ready for seeding. Make sure that the grass seed used will produce matching turf, and protect the area during recovery.

STAGNANT AREAS

On old, rather neglected lawns it is common to find areas where the drainage is poor, or where the surface has become sealed by hard use and water is held just below the surface. A build-up of undecayed root fibre acting as a sponge can have a similar effect. The easiest way to deal with such areas is hollow-tine aeration. Fine charcoal or sharp

Right: *If the edge is badly damaged or overgrown by spreading garden plants, it is best to cut it back to a new line. Use an edging iron with a straight plank as a guide.*

gritty sand is worked down the core holes to create short but effective vertical drains.

Above: *Suckers sprouting from tree roots beneath the lawn can only be cured by exposing and chopping out the whole root.*

WEED PATCHES

Renovating a weed or moss-infested lawn is best attempted in spring or early autumn, depending on the weather. Use a suitable selective weedkiller to kill the weeds or moss, then give the lawn a good raking or brushing to see how much grass has survived. Any coarse grasses can be grubbed out by hand, or spot-treated with a grass killer. As you go, fill any holes with a mixture of soil, peat and sand.

No sooner than six weeks after using the selective weedkiller, the lawn can be reseeded. If necessary, apply a spring or autumn fertiliser about a week before sowing; it is also worth giving the surface a good pricking with a garden fork or aerating machine. Broadcast the seed at ½-1oz per yd^2 (17-34g per m^2), work it in with the back of a rake, and cover it with ⅛-¼in (3-6mm) of potting compost. A light rolling will bed the seed in.

Once the young grass has germinated, let it develop a good root system before doing any more to it. Don't be impatient; even if the renovation is started in the autumn there is usually time to mow the new grass a few times before the winter weather sets in. Be sure the mower blades are sharp and that the machine is set high.

This treatment will not see the end of the weeds, but it will provide a good basis for further improvement. As more weeds come through, treat them with selective or spot herbicides as appropriate, and fill up any holes with compost. Eventually, if you are diligent, the renovated lawn will be indistinguishable from one which was never allowed to deteriorate.

COMMON LAWN WEEDS

Weeds are usually the first plants to appear on the site of a new lawn. They may have been growing on the site for years, or digging may have disturbed seeds lying dormant in the soil. Other weeds may come in from outside the garden, to flourish amid the new grasses and on old, patchy turf.

All lawn weeds have to be able to tolerate mowing. Some have compact leaf rosettes which escape the blades, while others have low creeping stems. Many of the perennials store plant food in tubers, bulbs or corms, underground stems (rhizomes) or surface-rooting creeping stems (stolons); such

Creeping buttercup
Ranunculus repens
A major lawn weed; it spreads by creeping stems which take root to form new plants. It has slightly hairy leaves, with three lobes each divided into three segments. Prefers moist, heavy soils. Treat with two doses of weedkiller.

Bulbous buttercup
Ranunculus bulbosus
Recognised by the corm-like growth at the base of the stem, this has leaves much like the creeping form but smaller. The flower stalks are hairy. It favours dry situations. Treat with repeated doses of weedkiller.

Lesser celandine
Ranunculus ficaria
Forms a rosette of long-stalked fleshy, shiny leaves, and star-shaped flowers in early spring. Spreads by creeping stems, and prefers shaded, moist locations. Difficult to kill: use repeated doses of weedkiller.

Pearlwort
Sagina procumbens
A very small plant with narrow leaves, which produces many stolons forming dense colonies of tiny rosettes, bearing minute white flowers. Common on all soils. Lawn sand will check it; otherwise use selective weedkiller.

plants can survive repeated close cutting, sprouting new foliage after every cut. This makes them very difficult to eradicate. Many of the annuals are less resilient, but given the chance they will seed prolifically and spread all over the garden.

Some weeds only become a problem in the lawn in certain soil conditions. Selfheal, for example, thrives on poorly-drained, heavy soils, whereas sheep's sorrel is normally found on dry, very acid soils. In such cases it is essential to use a grass seed mixture suited to the soil type, otherwise the weeds will prosper where the grasses fail.

Mouse-ear chickweeds
Cerastium *species*
A group of annuals and perennials, with pairs of hairy, greyish-green oval leaves. Widespread, particularly on soils lacking essential nutrients for grasses. Use one dose of weedkiller, or control with lawn sand.

Parsley piert
Aphanes arvensis
A small, creeping annual weed of dry soils, which may produce several generations each year. It has fan-shaped parsley-like leaves and bears clusters of minute green flowers. Treat with a weed-killer containing ioxynil.

Cat's-ear
Hypochaeris radicata
Often confused with dandelion, Cat's-ear forms rosettes of oblong, round-lobed leaves, green above and blue-green below. The whole plant is covered with short, stiff hairs. It may take two applications of weedkiller to eradicate it.

Yarrow
Achillea millefolium
A very strongly creeping plant with rhizomes, fern-like leaves, and white or pinkish flowers, able to resist drought conditions that kill many grasses. It prefers dry soils. Difficult to kill, it will survive many doses of weedkiller.

COMMON LAWN WEEDS

You may unwittingly create conditions which discourage grass and invite weeds to grow. Mowing too close can harm the grasses, allowing such surface-hugging plants as pearlwort and parsley piert to become established. Too much phosphorous in spring fertiliser will encourage clovers, and a shortage of humus (remedied by top-dressing) may result in infestations of yarrow or wood-rush. If you allow grass plants to die for lack of water during a dry summer, small bare patches will be created; when the drought ends the weeds will take over before the grasses have a chance to fill the gap.

Selfheal
Prunella vulgaris
A perennial which has rhizomes and creeping stems which root at intervals. It has purple flowers and stalked, spade-shaped leaves with deep veins. It favours heavy soils and wet situations. Repeated doses of weedkiller may be needed.

Sheep's sorrel
Rumex acetosella
A small plant which has creeping stems and slender, waisted leaves with prominent spreading lobes at the base. It occurs on poor, light, dry acid soils. Two applications of weedkiller in late spring will usually deal with the problem.

White clover
Trifolium repens
A creeping plant which can cover large areas of lawn. Each leaf has three leaflets marked with a pale inverted V. It is widespread, and particularly common on alkaline soils. Lawn sand will control it, or weedkiller.

Dandelions
Taraxacum officinale
A very variable plant; usually the leaves are smooth (but sometimes downy or bristly), and deeply toothed with backward-pointing triangular lobes. Common on all soils, it is easily controlled with weedkillers.

Every lawn will suffer from the occasional weed, but if the grass is healthy and growing well, the problem will never become severe. To discourage weeds, keep the turf properly fed and watered, mow it regularly, and ensure that the drainage and aeration are adequate. If the lawn develops any bare patches, re-seed or re-turf them before they are colonised by intruders. Keep a sharp watch for creeping stems invading the lawn from adjacent garden plots or paths, and if the lawn already has weeds, always use a grass box on the mower to collect the clippings and prevent the spread of seeds.

Daisy
Bellis perennis
The flowers, white or pink with a yellow centre, rise from flat rosettes of oval leaves with notched edges. Often tolerated, it can become a major problem on any soil. Use lawn sand to control it, or one or two doses of weedkiller.

Speedwells
Veronica *species*
A group of plants with small, four-petalled blue or mauve flowers. The commonest lawn species are germander speedwell (illustrated) and slender speedwell, a perennial which forms large mats. Control with weedkiller containing ioxynil.

Plantains
Plantago *species*
A large group of plants, very variable in leaf shape. Some have strap-like leaves, others oval and one, starweed, has deeply-divided narrow leaves. They are easily controlled with selective weedkillers.

Field woodrush
Luzula campestris
Often mistaken for a grass, woodrush can be recognised by its very hairy leaves and conspicuous tuft of hairs in the crown of the plant. It prefers drier soils, and is difficult to kill: use repeated doses of weedkiller.

DEALING WITH WEEDS

Weeds may invade any lawn, however well-managed. Some are killed by repeated mowing, or may be easily pulled up by hand. Most will also respond to chemical treatment, using either lawn sand or selective weedkillers.

HAND WEEDING

Newly-seeded lawns usually bear a fine crop of weeds, but it can be dangerous to use chemicals in case they harm the young grass plants. Luckily the weeds are usually easy to pull out, although you should take care not to disturb the lawn surface too much. Hold down the surrounding soil with your hand and pull the weeds out between your fingers.

As the lawn matures the weeds are not so easy to get out; the roots get a firm grip in the turf, and a straight pull will often leave pieces of root in the soil which may develop into new plants. In such cases it is better to dig the weed out with a hand fork, taking care to collect every part of the plant. If there are more than a few isolated weeds it may be better to use a weedkiller.

Weed grasses are not affected by selective weedkillers, which are formulated to kill weeds and leave the grass plants unscathed. One way of dealing with some coarse grasses which invade the lawn is to use an edging iron to cut through the foliage and roots at ground level. Large patches of weed grass should be dug out, and the gaps filled with clean soil and re-seeded.

LAWN SAND

Ferrous sulphate mixed with sand is a well-established treatment for lawn weeds. The grains fall off the vertical grass blades but settle on the broad, rough leaves of the weeds; the herbicide then scorches the foliage and quickly destroys it. The roots are not affected, and many weeds spring up again from the remains; repeated dressings may be needed. Even so, lawn sand has its advantages. It controls a broad range of weeds, and will even kill mosses; also the inclusion of ammonium sulphate—a nitrogen compound—in the mixture inhibits the growth of clover and "greens up" the grass.

Lawn sand is best applied in late spring at a rate of 2oz per yd^2 (67g per m^2). Spread it evenly, then stay off the lawn until it rains—if it doesn't rain

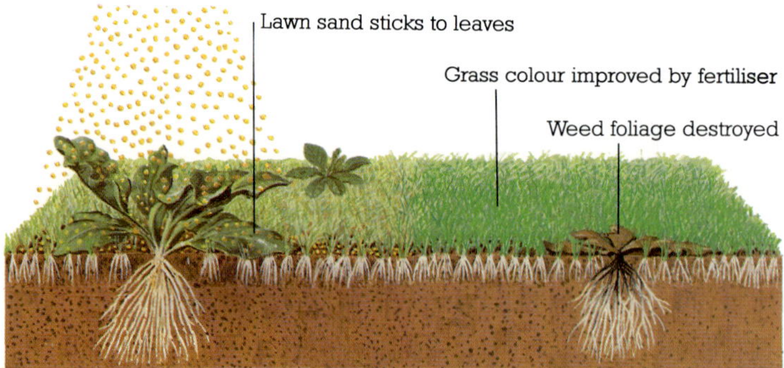

Above: *Lawn sand is a mixture of sand, weedkiller and fertiliser. When sprinkled on the lawn it collects on the broad leaves of the weeds (left), rapidly destroying the foliage but leaving the roots unaffected (right). The heavy grains do not stick to the grass blades, but fall through to the ground.*

within two days water the grass thoroughly to wash the dressing into the soil. After 20 days or so, rake the debris out of the lawn, and if necessary repeat the application.

SELECTIVE WEEDKILLER

Lawn sand is an effective way of keeping a good lawn in condition, but it is not powerful enough for badly infested lawns or very stubborn weeds. The best way to deal with these is to use a selective weedkiller. There are many types available; most contain two or three active ingredients to broaden the range of weeds they affect, but all are harmless to grass if used in the right quantities. Their main advantage is that the chemical is absorbed by the weed, enters the sap and flows to every growing part of the plant—including the roots. Their disadvantage is that they take a long time to act, and it may be six weeks before the weeds are destroyed.

To use, first select a product which is appropriate to your problem. For example, some weeds such as speedwell are unaffected unless the weedkiller contains ioxynil. Most products are applied in liquid form, or sometimes mixed with a fertiliser. Choose a day when the grass is dry and there is no wind—if the liquid is blown on to garden plants it will kill them. For the same reason it is best not to use a sprayer in a small garden as spray cannot be easily controlled; use a watering can fitted with a fine rose or weeder bar. Apply the liquid evenly, following the manufacturer's instructions, and remember that too much may damage the lawn you are trying to improve. One dose is usually enough, but some weeds may need a second after about six weeks.

TAKE CARE!

- Keep children and pets off the lawn during and immediately after treatment
- Keep weedkiller away from fish
- Wash hands and face after using weedkiller
- Wash all equipment after use and reserve it for weedkiller. Never water garden plants from a contaminated container.
- Store chemicals well away from children, animals and plants
- Do not keep chemicals in unmarked or wrongly-marked bottles

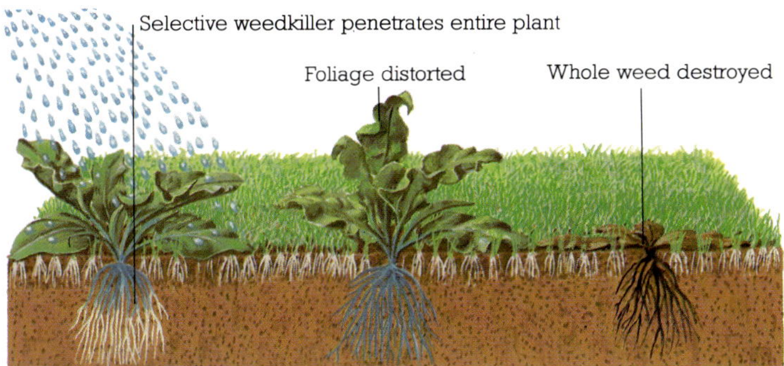

Above: *When selective weedkiller is absorbed by the leaves of a weed (left) it is transported to all parts of the plant and disrupts its growth pattern. At first the plant grows faster, causing distortion of the leaves (centre) but after some weeks both leaves and roots die and rot away (right).*

LAWN PESTS

However carefully you may treat your lawn, it is difficult to protect the grasses from attack or damage by animals. Many creatures which inhabit the soil depend on parts of the plant for food, particularly the root system. Other animals, such as moles and earthworms, disfigure the lawn with piles of soil dug out from beneath the turf.

EARTHWORMS

Earthworms can be a nuisance on the lawn, for they produce wormcasts which may smother and even kill the fine lawn grasses. The casts also often contain weed seeds brought up from the lower levels, which germinate easily in their ready-made seedbeds.

Very few worm species actually produce casts at the surface, but any attempt to control them may affect the whole earthworm population; if there are no worms the soil will suffer. It is best to avoid control measures unless the wormcast problem becomes acute. Some temporary control can be effected with irritants such as potassium permanganate dissolved in water at a rate of 1oz to the gallon per yd^2 (32g to 5 litres per m^2), or derris dust applied dry at about 1oz per yd^2 (35g per m^2) and watered in. A more drastic treatment is to use chlordane or carbaryl, both available as branded wormkillers.

CUTWORMS

The caterpillars of certain night-flying moths can cause considerable damage to lawn grasses. They are known as cutworms because they eat the grass after cutting their way through the stems almost at soil level. Sevin dust or HCH dust is usually an effective treatment.

LEATHERJACKETS

These greyish-brown grubs hatch from eggs laid in late summer or autumn by the cranefly. Their staple diet is the root of the grass plant. Feeding voraciously, they reach a length of about 1in (25mm) and then pupate; they emerge as craneflies the following summer or autumn.

You can test for leatherjackets by laying a wet sack on the lawn and leaving it overnight; the grubs, if present, will probably be found on the surface when the sack is removed. Heavily infested turf soon loses colour and becomes spongy as the grubs devour the root system, and if there are many craneflies around in the autumn, it is good policy to treat the turf with sevin dust or HCH.

CHAFER GRUBS

There are many types of chafer grub, and most can cause damage to grassland. The chief

Above: *Earthworms are invaluable in the garden, aerating and improving the soil, but their casts can ruin the lawn.*

Above: *Cutworms (left) eat grass foliage, and may cause a lot of damage. Ants (right) make small soil heaps but do little harm.*

offender is the garden chafer, or June bug (*Phyllopertha horticola*). Swarms of a thousand or more may descend on small areas to lay their eggs. These hatch into creamy-white six-legged grubs with glossy brown heads, which live underground and gnaw at the roots of the grass plant. They can be dealt with using the chemicals recommended for leatherjackets.

BIBIO GRUBS

Several members of the Bibionidae family—black, hairy flies often found on manure and compost heaps—develop from grubs which inhabit the lawn. Although not as destructive as leatherjackets they are often present in large numbers and can cause considerable damage. The treatment is the same as for leatherjackets and chafer grubs.

MOLES

If moles take a liking to the garden they can ruin the lawn, tunnelling beneath it to create ridges and troughs in the surface, and piling up soil into molehills. The best policy, if there are moles about, is to make the lawn unattractive to them by controlling the worms and grubs which form their food. Smoke canisters for fumigating mole tunnels are available, but they should be used with caution. Trapping and poisoning are extreme remedies, and must not be attempted by the amateur.

ANTS

Although ants may be a nuisance, they do very little harm on the lawn. They remove soil from around the grass roots, which in dry weather can cause stress to the plants; they may also produce heaps of soil at the surface. If the problem is serious, use an ant killer, but be sure it is safe to use on turf.

RABBITS

Apart from disfiguring the lawn with their droppings, and causing discoloured patches with their urine, rabbits can nibble the grass so closely that it is almost defoliated. They are very difficult to control; there are no suitable chemical measures, and if the problem is severe, wire-mesh rabbit fencing round the garden may be the only answer.

DOGS

In general dogs do no harm, but bitch urine can cause burnt yellow-brown patches on the lawn. The only remedy is several buckets of water applied as promptly as possible to dilute the urine and wash it through to a lower level—or, of course, keep the animal off the lawn.

Above: *Leatherjackets (left) and bibio grubs (right) are easier to kill than chafers (centre), for they live nearer the surface.*

Above: *If a mole is attracted by worms and grubs beneath the lawn it will soon undermine all your hard work.*

GRASS DISEASES

Turf which has been damaged or weakened by over-use, blunt mower blades or improper feeding is very vulnerable to fungus disease. Discoloured patches appear in the lawn as the fungi feed on the plants, and if the disease is not checked the grass often dies.

RED THREAD

Close inspection of irregularly shaped patches of straw-coloured grass reveals clearly visible red threads attached to the leaves; the blades may also be bound together in pinkish clusters. This disease may attack at any time of year, and the red threads can be accidentally carried from place to place, spreading the infection. It is often associated with a shortage of nitrogen; good lawn care and sufficient feeding should prevent it, while fungicides containing dichlorophen will treat it.

FUSARIUM PATCH

This is probably the commonest and most damaging of the fungal diseases—the affected areas die in a few days at most. The disease appears as small circular moist patches, 1-2in (25-50mm) in diameter, sometimes with a white or pinkish cottony mould. In time they grow larger, turn yellow and then orange-brown, before the total collapse of the attacked plants. The disease is often associated with humid conditions, and affects lawns with sealed, poorly-drained upper layers. The infection is easily carried from place to place. It should be treated with fungicide containing benomyl.

DOLLAR SPOT

Usually confined to lawns from coastal turf, this may be carried from such areas to cause trouble on other lawns. Affected grass turns yellow or golden (hence the name) in patches 2-3in (50-75mm) across, and the patches often join together to form large areas of dead, strawlike grass. Prompt treatment with benomyl is essential to contain an attack.

TAKE-ALL

A common disease of cereal crops, equally common among the bent grasses (*Agrostis*) but rare on fescues. Large patches of turf collapse, up to 39in (1m) across, and the outer rim of the area assumes a yellow-orange hue. The lawn grasses die,

Below: *Red thread disease on the lawn is easily identified by the red strands among the dying, straw-coloured grass.*

and immune grasses and weeds take their place. The disease frequently attacks turf on naturally acid soils after liming, and is very difficult to control short of cutting out the affected patches. The entire root system and surrounding soil should be removed, since the disease is largely soil-borne.

POWDERY MILDEW

An aptly-named disease which attacks many grass species. Affected plants have a powdery appearance and change colour from green to buff, and on to brown and finally yellow. Once again a fungicide containing benomyl is the answer.

Above: *Golden spots merging to form strawlike patches, but with no visible fungus, indicate an attack of dollar spot.*

ANTHRACNOSE

Normally associated with annual meadow grass, this disease starts with yellowing of the leaf tip; the effect then spreads down the leaf and stem to the centre of the plant, which becomes orange or orange-red. It is caused by compaction at the surface preventing proper drainage; if this is corrected there will be no need for fungicidal treatment.

DAMPING OFF

This only affects seedling grasses, which rapidly change from green to red or brown, collapse and die. The disease spreads extremely rapidly, and since it occurs in the early days of seed germination it is possible to lose an entire sowing in a matter of hours. It often occurs where the sward is overcrowded with seedlings owing to the sowing rate being too heavy. Cheshunt Compound is the most effective treatment.

Below: *Fusarium patch appears as a cottony mould in early morning and forms collapsed brown patches by evening.*

MOSSES, ALGAE, LICHENS AND FUNGI

If the lawn is neglected it may be invaded by mosses, lichens and other plants which can tolerate poor conditions. Most are easily killed, but the underlying causes must be remedied to prevent the problem recurring.

MOSS

Mosses are very common in grassland, and are well adapted to survival in the lawn. They need very little light, and are at their strongest in autumn and winter when the grasses may well be at low ebb. They are also extremely resistant to drought. Mosses have no proper root system—they are anchored to the soil by small rhizoids which function like root hairs, taking in nutrients from the surface.

There are two main types found on the lawn. The acrocarps are found in very poor soils and in conditions created by mowing too closely; they form dense mats of tightly-packed leaves. The other group, known as the pleurocarps, are very much more open in growth, with feathery foliage. All mosses produce spores instead of seeds, and they are able to reproduce vegetatively; fragments of the leaves, stems and even single rhizoids are capable of producing entire plants. For this reason you should never rake out the living moss unless you want to spread it.

There are four main reasons for mossy lawns—soil compaction, excessive moisture at the surface, soil impoverishment and over-acidity. Unless the basic fault is corrected the moss will recur despite treatment. Find the problem and remedy it before using a mosskiller. When the moss is dead it can be raked out, and the lawn reseeded if necessary.

ALGAE

Various forms of algae may occur if the lawn surface is always damp. Algae are simple plants with no roots or internal vein systems, and most types will only thrive in moist situations. They usually appear in shaded places as black, rather slippery masses which absorb moisture and swell to jelly-like blobs. If the basic cause is corrected the algae will disappear from the lawn without chemical treatment, but if necessary a fungicide can be used.

Above: *Mosses can completely overrun lawns in poor condition.* **Below:** *The lichen* Peltigera canina, *found under trees.*

Above: *A fairy ring is merely the visible part of an extensive underground fungus which spreads well beyond the ring itself.*

LICHENS

A lichen is a compound organism composed of an alga and a fungus; the two obtain food by different methods, feeding one another, and because of this lichen is able to grow in a variety of unpromising places, such as roof tiles and gravestones. On the lawn *Peltigera canina* (dog lichen) often occurs in the shade of trees, or where there is an excessive build-up of fibre causing poverty of the surface soil. It appears as leaf-like growths, almost black on top and curling to display a whitish underside. Another, *Collema pulposum,* occurs as jelly-like greenish-black masses, and is usually indicative of poor drainage.

Mosses, algae and lichens are immune to selective weed-killers, but they can be kept in check by using ferrous sulphate at ½oz per yd² (17g per m²), mixed with water to ensure even application. Lawn sand, which has the same active ingredient, can also be used. For complete eradication, however, the basic fault in the lawn should be corrected.

FAIRY RINGS

The fairy ring is produced by the fungus *Marasmius oreades* and its relatives. The toadstools which appear at the surface do no harm, but the underground mycelium—a waxlike network of fine white threads—spreads among the grass roots and stops the normal passage of moisture through the soil. The grass plants are deprived of food, and die. The mycelium spreads outward annually and so the ring grows larger; eventually the grass may regrow at the centre.

Fairy rings are very stubborn, and will only yield to specialised chemical treatments or physical removal. This involves cutting out the affected area, including an 18in (half-metre) band round the outside, and removing all the soil affected by the mycelium—this is clearly visible and has an unpleasant smell. The hole should be refilled with fresh soil and the area returfed.

Puffballs and field mushrooms may produce strips, rings or partial rings of dark-coloured grass, because of the nitrogen released by the mycelium. Neither of these fungi kill the grass in the same way as the true fairy ring, and they can be controlled by using the ferrous sulphate treatment recommended for algae and lichens.

Equipment

An efficient, well-maintained mower is an essential tool for any lawn owner, but it is only one of a range of turf maintenance equipment. Many make light work of jobs which are otherwise neglected, and the initial investment is usually well repaid by the improved appearance and texture of the lawn.

MOWERS

Traditional lawnmowers cut the grass using the scissor action of a cylinder of blades revolving against a fixed bottom blade. The simplest type is the hand sidewheel mower, supported by two wheels which drive the blades. Such machines are fine for small areas, but mowing right up to a properly-cut lawn edge is difficult, and the machine does not create the striped effect which many prefer.

Stripes are produced by cylinder machines which incorporate back rollers. The roller flattens the cut grass in the direction of travel, so mowing up and down the lawn results in bands of grass flattened in opposite directions, creating the stripes.

Cylinder machines do not cope well with wet or long grass. They also need careful maintenance, because their efficiency depends upon the sharpness and precise adjustment of the blades. Despite these problems, the high quality of cut produced by such a well-adjusted machine has made the type very popular.

Lightweight electric mowers with horizontally-rotating blades are now among the most widely-used machines, because they are easy to use and less sensitive to poor conditions than cylinder types. If the blade is sharp, they will cut quite long grass, even when it is wet, and blade adjustment is simple. The finish produced by a rotary cannot be compared with that of a well-adjusted cylinder mower, but it is quite good enough for a utility lawn. Models are now available with rollers fitted—to make stripes—and grass cutting collection systems.

Below: *A cylinder mower with a back roller gives a very good finish, shearing the grass between a fixed bottom blade and a rotating blade cylinder.*

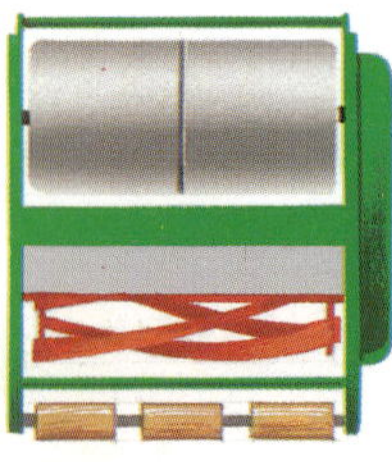

The hover mower is basically a rotary with a fan fitted on the spindle above the blade, arranged to blow downwards. This creates an air cushion inside the hood—like a hovercraft—causing the mower to float over the lawn surface touching only the leaf-tips of the grass. These are sliced off by the rotary blade. Such mowers will cut wet or dry grass equally well, and float over undulating ground without damaging the turf. They even make light work of quite steep banks when used as directed by the manufacturer. A hover mower will not leave a striped effect, however, for it has no roller.

POWER SUPPLY

A hand-driven cylinder mower is still a good choice for a small lawn. There is less to go wrong, no problems with cables, and many gardeners enjoy the exercise.

Electric mains-powered machines are light, dependable and efficient, and ideal for moderate-sized lawns which are no more than 200ft (60m) from a power point at the farthest corner. If the cable is longer than this it can overheat and become dangerous. Cylinder, rotary and hover types are available.

Battery-powered rechargeable electric mowers are little used today. Free of trailing cables, they are not limited by distance from the power point, but the weight of the battery makes them more cumbersome than mains-powered machines.

Petrol-engined mowers are more expensive than their electric counterparts, but they are sturdy and powerful, and ideal for large lawns and heavy-duty work. Cylinder, rotary and hover designs are available in a variety of cutting widths, and many models are self-propelled. For very large areas there are ride-on petrol mowers—cylinder types with trailing seats for a fine finish, or rotary types resembling small tractors which will deal with long, coarse grass.

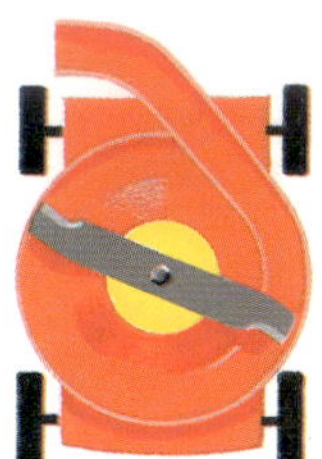

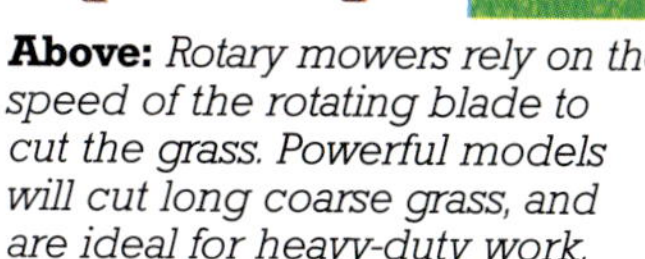

Above: *Rotary mowers rely on the speed of the rotating blade to cut the grass. Powerful models will cut long coarse grass, and are ideal for heavy-duty work.*

Below: *A hover mower floats on a cushion of air created by a fan above the blade, and will glide harmlessly over uneven or vulnerable lawn surfaces.*

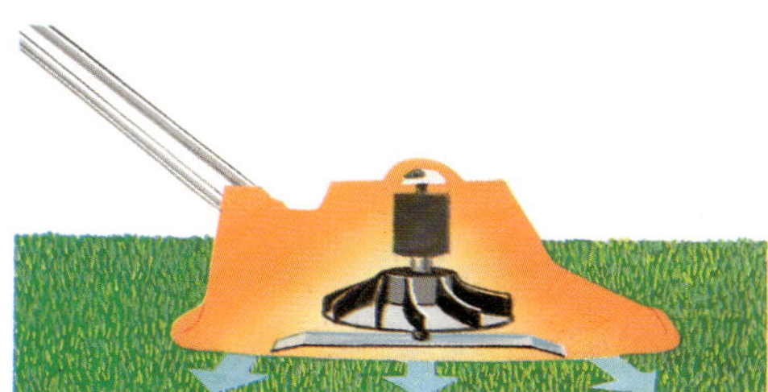

MOWER MAINTENANCE

Before the mower is put away for the winter it should be cleaned, serviced and protected against corrosion. If the machine is in good condition the work should pose no problems for the practical gardener, and the effort will be rewarded by many years of efficient service.

CYLINDER MOWERS

If the blades are not too badly notched or distorted they can be sharpened by a process known as back lapping—turning the cylinder of blades backwards to grind them against the fixed bottom blade. The cylinder must be adjusted so that the clearance is very tight, and dressed with some coarse-grade grinding paste before turning the blades by hand using the roller or drive mechanism. Don't risk your fingers by turning the blades directly. As the grinding proceeds further adjustment will be necessary to keep the moving and fixed blades in contact. When the blades are sharp—they should cut paper cleanly—readjust the cylinder to increase the clearance a little, and wash off all the grinding paste; if it gets into the bearings the mower will be ruined. Make sure that the bottom blade is in good condition, or the back lapping technique will fail miserably; if it is badly worn, replace it.

Using a really stiff brush with soapy water or a mild solution of detergent, clean down the paintwork and remove all plant debris from the mechanism and the delivery plate which curves over the cylinder. There are chemical aerosol cleaners available which also give excellent results. Wipe down all chains and mechanical parts with a rag, and apply a light dressing of oil. Make sure all the bearings are properly lubricated, and oil if necessary.

Above: *Clear all plant debris off the mechanism and blades.*

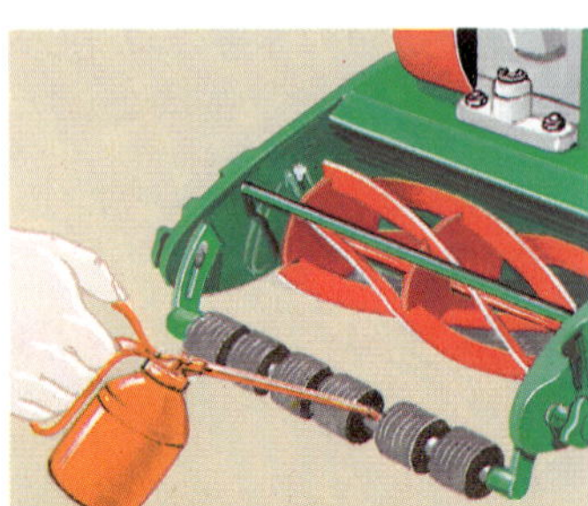

Above: *Oil all bearings and exposed metal parts.*

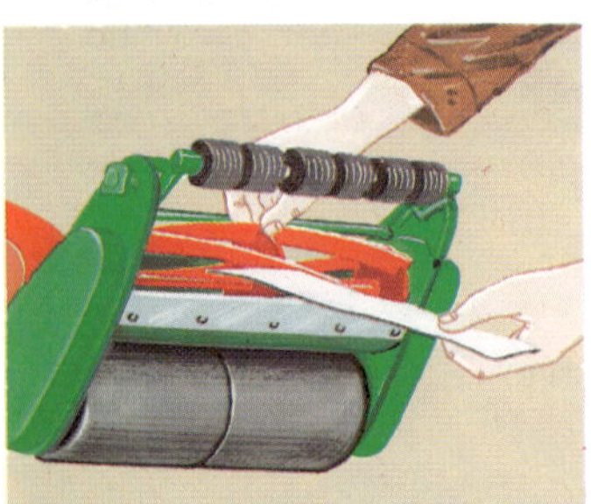

Above: *If the blades are sharp they will cut paper cleanly.*

Above: *Check the adjustment of the mowing height and blades.*

ROTARY MOWERS

Maintaining a rotary mower is relatively simple. There are fewer moving parts to care for, and the cutting efficiency does not rely on accurate adjustment of the blade. Even so, the blade must be sharp. If it is in good condition, it can be sharpened using a file on the bevelled edge. You may have to take it off the mower to do this. A badly-notched blade will need the edge recutting on a grindstone—a job for a professional—or may need to be replaced.

Many rotary mowers are made largely of plastic, so they will not go rusty like metal-bodied machines. Nevertheless they still benefit from a good scrub with a stiff brush, both inside and outside the hood, to remove accumulated grass cuttings and sap. Check that the area round the central bearing is free of debris, and on a hover mower make sure that the fan is not clogged.

Above: *Use a file or stone to sharpen a rotary blade.*

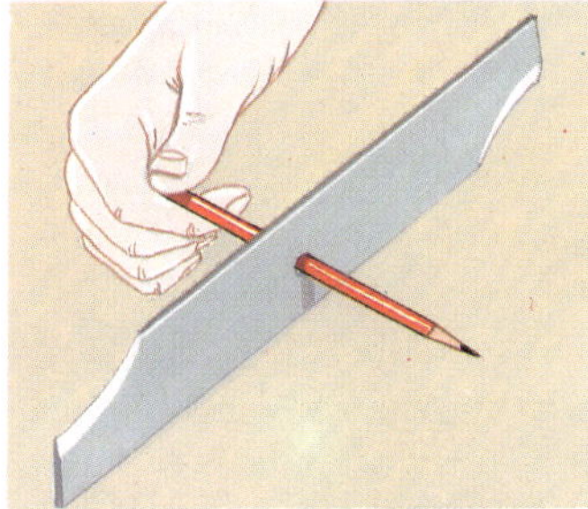

Above: *Check the balance of a rotary blade after sharpening.*

PETROL ENGINES

Check the cooling fins for plant debris and clean them by careful brushing. Clean the air filter as directed by the manufacturer; some are made of foam and can be washed in a detergent solution, thoroughly (but slowly) dried and then given a spot of oil before replacing. All ventilation holes or grids must be thoroughly cleaned, paying special attention to the air intake of the carburettor.

Take the spark plug out and check that it is in good condition. Serious damage indicates something wrong with the engine, and a job for a mechanic. If all is well, clean the electrodes with a fine wire brush and check the gap with a feeler gauge (normally 0·5mm).

ELECTRIC MOWERS

Most electric motors on mowers are sealed units which require little more than general cleaning at the end of the season. An old motor may have worn brushgear—refer to the maker's instructions for details of checking and replacement. Check all connections and insulation, and on mains-powered machines examine the cable and plugs carefully for damage. If the mower is battery-powered make sure the battery is charged before the onset of winter, remove it from the mower and store it in a reasonably warm, dry place. Ensure that the battery plates are covered with distilled water.

TAKE CARE!

When working on a motor mower make sure the power source is disconnected. Take off the spark plug lead, unplug the mains cable, or unscrew the battery lead before doing anything else.

LAWNCARE TOOLS

It is possible to make and maintain a fine lawn using only the simplest general-purpose tools, but the work can be done much more quickly and efficiently using specially-designed lawn maintenance equipment.

EDGING TOOLS

A good sharp pair of long-handled edging shears are essential for trimming the grass at the edge of the lawn, even if you use a mechanical edge trimmer for most of the work. The shears can be used in tighter corners, and will deal with neglected edges more effectively than mechanical trimmers. The other basic edging tool is the half-moon edging iron, which is used vertically, like a spade, to cut away damaged turf from the edge.

Mechanical trimmers usually have star-shaped rotary blades which act against a fixed blade to cut off overhanging grass. The motorised models are the most efficient for heavy use, and for the owner of a large lawn such a tool is a good investment.

SPRAYERS AND WATERING CANS

Weed control eventually becomes necessary on most lawns, and today the job is normally done with selective weedkillers, which have to be applied as a fine spray. The knapsack-type sprayer fitted with a hand lance is most effective for large areas, but for smaller areas it is best to use a watering can fitted with a spraybar attachment. Although slower, it is easier to control than a large sprayer, and there is less risk of spray drift.

Once a can or sprayer has been used for weedkiller it may be contaminated for life, so it must never be used for any other purpose. Reserve it for weedkiller and mark it clearly.

Above: *An alternative to the traditional edging iron is a simple knife trimmer which is pushed along the lawn edge.*

Above: *A manual rotary edge trimmer is quicker than shears but it will only work well if the edge is well-maintained.*

HOSES AND SPRINKLERS

A hosepipe is essential for lawn irrigation during the summer. There are now space-saving hoses available which collapse flat before being wound on to a slim reel, and these are perhaps the easiest to clear of water, clean and store. The orthodox non-flattening hose is stronger, particularly if it is of the reinforced type, but it needs to be carefully drained and stored on a bulky reel to prevent leaks developing.

Although the hosepipe can be fitted with a rose for watering the flower beds or vegetable plots, this method is not suitable for the lawn. You will need a good lawn sprinkler, either the single-spike type which sends up a broken stream of water to fall

Above: *A spring-tine rake is an essential lawn tool, ideal for collecting leaves and raking out thatch and dead moss.*

Above: *A hand-operated hollow-tine aerator is a simple but effective device which will improve a compacted lawn.*

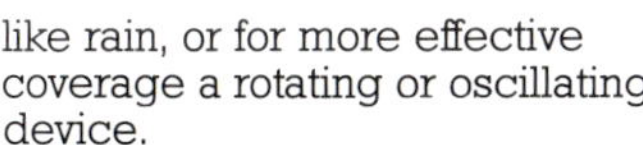

like rain, or for more effective coverage a rotating or oscillating device.

FERTILISER DISTRIBUTORS

These come in a variety of shapes and sizes. Some are simple containers with apertures in the base, either hand-held or mounted on wheels. They merely allow the dressing to fall through the gap, and depend for accurate spreading density on the user walking forward at the correct speed. The more complex powered distributors can be used at any speed to apply a wide range of fertilisers.

SCARIFIERS AND AERATORS

Scarifiers are designed to keep the lawn surface open, allowing air, moisture and fertilisers to pass into the soil. The simplest are the various brooms and rakes—all very effective but tiring to use on a large area. A mechanised scarifier is a very practical alternative for a big lawn.

An aerator is used when deeper penetration is needed, allowing air to reach the soil beneath the turf. The simplest aerator is the garden fork, but a hand-operated hollow-tine aerator, which takes out cores of soil, is more effective. Both these techniques can prove hard work, however, and there are a variety of mechanised devices—some with interchangeable tines for different problems—which are either hand-pushed or motorised. The powered types are the most efficient.

Above: *Slit-tine aerators have blades which slice into the soil and prune the roots, encouraging new growth.*

Above: *A solid-tine aerator is a mechanical version of the garden fork, less thorough but much quicker to use.*

Seasonal Care

There are very few weeks in the year when there is nothing to do on the lawn. In many areas the grass keeps growing all year round, and always needs attention. When the grass is not growing vigorously, there are always other plants and animals ready to move in and take over; the gardener has to be constantly on guard against weeds, soil pests and fungus diseases, and the conditions which encourage them.

AUTUMN AND WINTER

The soil is normally at its warmest in late summer and very early autumn, making this the best time of year to establish a new lawn from seed or turf. It is also possible to carry out general renovation work, but it is rather late to use selective weedkillers, and the need to mow the grass—which will be growing still—can make large-scale renovation very inconvenient.

Healthy root development should be encouraged by applying a phosphorous-rich autumn feed, after aerating the lawn using slit tines or hollow tines which prune the roots and promote new growth. As the season advances, and the grass needs mowing less and less frequently, the time is ideal for top-dressing with peat, leafmould or compost.

Clear all fallen leaves from the lawn, or they will encourage worm activity. This may be good for the soil, but too many worm-casts will disfigure the lawn and smother the grasses. Brush the leaves up and use them for compost. It is best not to add them to other compost materials, because they will slow down decomposition, so build a separate heap. In time they will decay into leafmould which makes an excellent top-dressing.

During the autumn months soil pests such as leatherjackets and chafer grubs can be a problem. Test for their presence by laying a wet sack on the lawn overnight; if any grubs are found under the sack in the morning, use an appropriate insecticide.

Patches of lawn in the shade will need aeration and a dressing of carbonate of lime, applied at 1-2oz per yd^2 (34-68g per m^2), to sweeten the surface. If the turf is sparse, scarify it and reseed with a mixture intended for shady places.

As autumn degenerates into winter the ground will often be too wet or frosty for work on the lawn, and it is better to stay off it. In a mild season, however, the grass may continue producing top-growth, and the occasional trim, with the cutters set high, will save trouble in the spring. It is best to use a hover mower for this, for the turf is nearly always damp and easily damaged.

If there is a risk of snow, a stiff brushing and an application of fungicide will prevent any possibility of Fusarium attack on grass trapped in a humid atmosphere under the snow layer.

Left: *Fallen leaves should be cleared from the lawn to discourage worm activity.*

SPRING AND SUMMER

It is surprising how much growth lawn grasses—even the finest varieties—can make during the winter, and the sooner regular mowing is resumed in the spring, the better. If the grass is rather long by the time you get on to it with the mower, don't be tempted to cut it closely or you may ruin the lawn for the rest of the year. Start with the mower set high and gradually reduce the height over the weeks to ½-¾in (13-19mm), depending on the quality of the grasses.

The lawn may need to be rolled lightly in early spring to resettle any turf laid the previous autumn, which has been lifted by winter frost. Normally the rest of the lawn will not need rolling, and the surface will need to be opened up rather than pressed down. Use a stiff brush or birch broom to lift the prostrate stems and loosen plant debris from the surface. Severe scarifying should not be necessary on a well-kept lawn, but gentle raking may be helpful. On large lawns it is quicker to use a mechanical leaf sweeper, which will both brush the lawn and gather up the debris. This is also a good time to carry out aeration, and spread top-dressing.

Left: *Regular irrigation during dry weather will keep the lawn green throughout the summer.*

Both moss and weeds in the lawn can be tackled in early spring. Apply mosskiller before doing any raking at all, and wait for the moss to die; if you rake out live moss you will merely spread the problem. If your lawn suffers from weeds, wait until the plants are actively growing before using selective weedkiller, taking care to avoid spray drift. Then, if weather and surface conditions allow, and the soil is warm enough for seed to germinate, there should be time for renovation and reseeding to produce a reasonable sward for the summer.

Having disposed of the weeds and moss, wait six weeks before sowing any seed. Lightly break the surface with a sharp-toothed rake to provide a key and, choosing a dry day, oversow the seed at ½-1oz per yd² (17-34g per m²), working the seed in and treading firm. Repair any broken edges and bare patches and reseed as necessary. Be alert to the possibility of damping-off disease on the seedling grass.

Once it is growing well the lawn will need a dressing of nitrogen-rich spring fertiliser to ensure healthy top-growth. The treatment can be repeated at half strength later in the season, if the grass needs it, but after mid-summer it is best to avoid using highly nitrogenous dressings.

As the grass approaches the flowering stage in late spring it will need frequent cutting. If this is neglected the grass plants will develop hard flowering stems which can create a mowing problem, particularly if you use a cylinder mower. If there is annual meadow grass in the lawn, brush the area before mowing to make the short flower-heads stand up; they will then be cut off by the mower blades and collected in the grassbox, if one is fitted.

If the weather is humid during the summer, watch for attacks of fungus disease, and the appearance of toadstools, lichens and algae. If the weather is very dry, start watering the lawn before the grass plants show obvious signs of strain. Be sure to give enough water, or you will encourage top-growth but not the root depth which the plants need to survive a drought. It is best to water in the evening during hot weather. Be careful with mowing during this period—the grass will be making relatively little top-growth and should not be cut too closely.

INDEX

A
Aeration 45, 48-9, 71
Agrostis grasses 16-17, 62
Algae 64
Alpine lawns 21
Alternatives to grass 20-1
Ammonium Sulphate 43
Annual meadowgrass 19, 63
Anthracnose 63
Ants 61
Autumn maintenance 36, 73

B
Battery-powered mowers 67
Bent grasses 16-17
Bibio grubs 60
Birds 32
Bitch urine 61
Bone Meal 43
Broken edges 52
Browntop 16
Brushing 48
Bulbous buttercup 54
Bumpy lawns 50-1
Button weed 21

C
Cat's-ear 55
Chafer grubs 60-1, 73
Chalky soils 22
Chamomile 21
Cheshunt Compound 63
Chewing's fescue 18
Clay soils 15, 23
Clippings 39
Clovers 20
Couch grass 19
Creeping bent 16-17
Creeping buttercup 54
Creeping grasses 15, 16, 46-7
Creeping red fescue 18
Creeping soft grass 19
Crested dogstail 18
Cultivation of site 28
Curving lawns 12-13
Cutting height 36
Cutworms 60
Cylinder mowers 37, 66, 67
  maintenance 68

D
Daisy 57
Damping-off disease 30, 32
  treatment for 63
Dandelions 56
Design 11-14
Diseases 62-3
Dogs 61
Dollar spot 62
Drainage 14, 24-5
Dried Blood 43

E
Earthworms 48, 60
Edges
  repairing 52
  trimming 35, 40-1
Edging strips 41
Edging tools 35, 40-1, 70
Electric mowers 39, 67
  maintenance 69
Equipment 66-71

F
Fairy rings 65
Feeding 42-5
  autumn 73
  spring 75
Fertiliser spreaders 42, 44, 71
Fertilisers 42-5
  pre-sowing 28, 30
Fescues 16, 18
Festuca grasses 16, 18
Field woodrush 57
Fine lawns 15
Fine-leaved fescue 18
Fusarium patch 62, 73

G
Grass clippings 39
Grasses 15, 16-19

H
Half-moon edging iron 35, 41, 70
Hand weeding 32, 58
  herb lawns 20
Hard fescue 18
Herb lawns 20-1
Hollow tining 49, 52, 71
Hollows 50-1
Hoof and horn meal 43
Hover mowers 35, 37, 39, 67
Humus 22

I
Irrigation 46-7, 75

K
Kentucky blue grass 17
Kidney weed 21

L
Landscaping 26-7
Lawn sand 58-9, 65
Lawn weeds 54-7
Leafmould 73
Leatherjackets 60, 73
Lesser celandine 54
Levelling 26-7
Lichens 65
Liquid fertilisers 44
Loams 23
Lolium grasses 16, 18

M
Machine tining 49, 71
Maintenance 36-65
  mowers 68-9
Manure, farmyard 28
Meadow grasses 16, 17
  annual 19, 63
Moles 61
Mosses 64, 75
Mouse-ear chickweeds 55
Mowers 37-9, 66-9
  maintenance 68-9
Mowing 36-9, 73, 74
  new lawns 31, 35
Muriate of Potash 43

N
Nitrogen 42, 43
NPK fertilisers 44

O
Ornamental lawns 15, 16
  mowing 36

P
Parsley piert 55
Paths 14
Pearlwort 54
Peat soils 22
Pennyroyal 21
Perennial ryegrass 18
Pests 60-1
Petrol mowers 38, 67
  maintenance 69
Phosphorous 42, 43
Pipes, drainage 25
Plantains 57
Play lawns 15, 36
Poa grasses 16, 17, 19
Potash 42, 43
Powdery mildew 63

R
Rabbits 61
Raking 48
  new lawn site 28-9
Red thread 62
Renovation 50-3, 75
Repairs 50-3
Reseeding 53, 75
Rotary mowers 37, 39, 66
  maintenance 69
Rough stalked meadow grass 17
Ryegrasses 16, 18

S
Safety measures
mowers, 39, 69
using weedkiller 59
Sandy soils 22
Scarifiers 48, 71
Seasonal care 72-5
Seed mixtures 16
Seeding 29-32
Selective weedkillers 20, 59
application 70
on neglected lawns 53
on new lawns 32
Selfheal 56
Shady sites 13, 29
Shape of lawn 12-13
Shears, edging 40-1, 70
Sheep's sorrel 56
Site preparation 24-9
Sloping sites 13
Slow-release fertilisers 44
Smooth stalked meadow grass 17
Soakaways 24
Soil types 14, 15, 22-3
testing 22
Speedwells 57
Sprayers 70
Spring maintenance 36, 74-5
Sprinklers 47, 71
Stagnant areas 52
Stepping-stone paths 14
Stony soils 23
Striped effect 39
Sulphate of Potash 43
Summer maintenance 36, 75
Superphosphate of lime 43

T
Take-all 62-3
Tamping tool 35
Terracing 13
Thyme, wild 21
Timothy grass 18
Tining 49
Top dressing 45, 73
uneven surfaces 50-1
Topsoil 22, 26, 28
Trace elements 42-4
Treading
new lawn site 28-9
Trees 13
Trenches 25
Trimmers, mechanical 41, 70
Tufted grasses 15, 16
Turfing 33-5

U
Uneven surfaces 50
Urea 43
Utility lawns 15, 16
mowing 36

W
Watering 46-7, 75
new lawns 32
Watering cans 70
Weed grasses 19
Weeding 53, 58-9
herb lawns 20
neglected lawns 53
new lawns 31-2
Weedkillers 20, 32, 53, 59
application 70
Weeds 54-7
in turf 34
White clover 56
Wild thyme 21
Winter maintenance 36, 73
Wormcasts 32, 48, 60

Y
Yarrow 20-1, 55
Yorkshire fog 19

PICTURE CREDITS

Artists
Copyright of the artwork illustrations on the pages following the artists' names is the property of Salamander Books Ltd.

Clifford and Wendy Meadway: 16, 25, 26, 28, 33, 40, 44, 45, 47, 51, 52, 53, 58, 59, 60-1
Colin Newman (Linden Artists): Front cover
Brian Watson (Linden Artists): 39, 66, 67, 68, 69, 70, 71

Photographs
The publishers wish to thank the following photographers, agencies and companies who have supplied photographs for this book. The photographs have been credited by page number and position on the page: (B) Bottom, (T) Top, (BL) Bottom Left etc.

Bruce Coleman Ltd: 57 (BR)
Eric Crichton: Endpapers, Title page, 6, 8-9, 10-11, 12, 13, 14-15, 17, 18-19, 24, 27, 29, 32 (T, C), 33, 34, 35, 37, 40, 41, 42, 46-7, 48, 49, 50, 51, 52-3, 54 (TL, TR), 55 (BL, BR), 56 (TL), 57 (TL, BL), 64 (T), 72-3, 74-5, Back cover
Flymo Ltd: 38
Murphy Chemical Ltd: 64 (B)
Bob Palin: 30-1, 32 (B)
Smith collection: 20, 21, 55 (TL), 56 (TR)
Synchemicals Ltd: 54 (BL, BR), 55 (TR), 56 (BL), 62, 63
John Woodward: 56 (BR), 57 (TR), 65

PRINTED IN BELGIUM BY
proost
INTERNATIONAL BOOK PRODUCTION